Relating Resources to Personnel Readiness

Use of Army Strength Management Models

John F. Schank
Margaret C. Harrell
Harry J. Thie
Monica M. Pinto
Jerry M. Sollinger

Prepared for the Office of the Secretary of Defense

National Defense Research Institute

RAND

Approved for public release; distribution unlimited

UA
25
.R45
1997

PREFACE

This report is the first installment of a project that examines the connection between resources and readiness. It investigates strength management and the role that two Army models play in it. The work was sponsored by the Deputy Under Secretary of Defense for Readiness, and was carried out in the Forces and Resources Policy Center of the National Defense Research Institute (NDRI), a federally funded research and development center sponsored by the Office of the Secretary of Defense, the Joint Staff, and the defense agencies. The work should interest those involved in readiness, the management of military personnel, or modeling of personnel functions.

CONTENTS

Preface	iii
Figures	vii
Tables	ix
Summary	xi
Acknowledgments	xvii
Acronyms	xix

Chapter One
INTRODUCTION	1
Background	1
Project Objective and Approach	3
Outline	3

Chapter Two
A FRAMEWORK FOR PERSONNEL READINESS	5
Personnel Readiness Is an Input to Overall Force Readiness	5
Certain Attributes Define Personnel Readiness	8
Various Activities Affect Personnel Readiness Attributes	10
Control and Response Variables Intermingle	10
Readiness Metrics	12
Initial Inventory of Personnel Models	13

Chapter Three
ARMY STRENGTH MANAGEMENT	17
Spaces	17
Faces	18

Operating Strength Deviation 18
Strength Management Is Modeled Because of
    Complexity 19
Strength Managers Have Modeling Choices 21
Models Are Part of a Process 23

Chapter Four
AN OVERVIEW OF ELIM AND MOSLS 25
ELIM Overview 25
ELIM General Analytic Approach and Architecture 27
MOSLS Overview 29
MOSLS General Analytic Approach and Architecture 31
Summary 32

Chapter Five
USING ELIM AND MOSLS TO RELATE RESOURCES TO
    PERSONNEL READINESS 35
Placing ELIM and MOSLS in the Personnel Readiness
    Framework 35
Placing ELIM and MOSLS in the Readiness Hierarchy 37
Cautions About Using ELIM and MOSLS to Relate
    Resources to Personnel Readiness 39
Personnel Readiness Attribute Levels and Sorts
    Measures 41
Extending the Research 43

Appendix
A.   DESCRIPTION OF ELIM 45
B.   DESCRIPTION OF MOSLS 63

References 81

FIGURES

S.1.	Where ELIM and MOSLS Fit	xiv
2.1.	Readiness Hierarchy	6
2.2.	The Relationship Between Attributes and Variables	11
2.3.	Framework for Personnel Readiness	12
4.1.	Relation of ELIM to Other Models and Databases	26
4.2.	ELIM Architecture	28
4.3.	Relation of MOSLS to Other Models and Databases	30
4.4.	MOSLS Architecture	31
5.1.	Where ELIM and MOSLS Fit	36
5.2.	ELIM and MOSLS Work in Both Directions	37
A.1.	Elim Is Key Part of Family of Strength Management Models	46
A.2.	Overview of ELIM Architecture	49
A.3.	Simulation Projects Inventory	55
A.4.	Objective Function and Optimization Criteria	58
B.1.	Relation of MOSLS to Other Models and Databases	64
B.2.	MOSLS Architecture	66
B.3.	Operation of Training Simulation Model	70
B.4.	Relationships Between Nodes and Arcs	72
B.5.	How the Model Uses Incentives	73
B.6.	Node and Arc Network of Trained Strength Model	75
B.7.	Trained Strength Model	77
B.8.	Reallocation of Original Accessions	78

TABLES

2.1. Initial Inventory of OSD and Service Personnel Models 14
A.1. Characteristic Groups Used for First-Term Personnel 50
B.1. MOSLS Rates and Factors 68

SUMMARY

CONNECTING RESOURCES TO READINESS

The end of the Cold War resulted in reduced force structures and diminished budgets, although the United States still faced a range of security challenges that was broader and more complex than those that had been posed by the Soviet Union. The more austere budget climate heightened policymakers' interest in the connection between resources and readiness. Fewer resources make it more important to ensure that they purchase the greatest capability possible.

This difficult task is made more so because resources do not connect directly to readiness. That is, it is not clear how much additional capability—or readiness—a given expenditure buys. How much more readiness does recruiting more people or buying more spare parts gain? The question has no easy answer, because readiness results from a complex interaction of many things, including people (their number and skills), equipment (amount on hand and its condition), command and control capabilities, strategic lift, and so forth.

The Office of the Secretary of Defense (OSD) and the Services have wrestled with this problem for years, attempting in various ways to characterize the readiness of forces. Currently in use is the SORTS system, which measures important components of readiness but provides something less than an accurate assessment.[1]

---

[1] SORTS—Status of Resources and Training System—is the readiness reporting system used by the Joint Staff. In it, the Services report on aspects of units relating to

CAN MODELS HELP?

The search for a more definitive link between resources and readiness has caused policymakers to look to models as a way of illuminating the connection. The specific task posed for this study was to identify, describe, and evaluate how well a model or set of models currently in use defines the connection between resources and readiness. We have undertaken that task, but we have broadened it beyond the description and evaluation of a set of models. We also consider how models might fit into the larger context of overall force readiness and what policymakers might have to do to improve their capability to assess that readiness.

Because people have such an important influence on readiness and because the Services use a rich array of models to manage personnel, we focused on the personnel function. Our search led us to two Army models: Enlisted Loss Inventory Model/Computation of Manpower Program using Linear Programming or ELIM,[2] and Military Occupational Specialty Level System or MOSLS.

ELIM is the primary model used by the Army to manage its enlisted personnel strength at the aggregate level. ELIM primarily addresses the enlisted personnel strength in operating units. It also tracks and produces output for the total Army end strength, including officers and personnel in the individuals account. Its primary function is to minimize the deviation between the number of people authorized and the number on hand.

The Army uses MOSLS to balance the Military Occupational Specialty (MOS) and grade-level requirements of the Army with the available population. It complements ELIM in that it provides grade and MOS detail, which ELIM does not consider. MOSLS supports enlisted personnel policy at two levels. At the most aggregate level, MOSLS enables Army analysts to explore the implications of policies and behaviors that affect the Service's need for total numbers of individuals with certain skills and grades. MOSLS also supports the

---

readiness: personnel, equipment, and training. They report by assigning numerical "C" (for "characteristic") ratings for each category and subcategory based on qualitative and quantitative criteria. For personnel, the services report on numbers assigned, skills, and grade.

[2]ELIM was formerly called ELIM-COMPLIP.

analysis of voluntary loss behavior and of involuntary loss policies upon the entire enlisted force. At the more detailed MOS and grade level, MOSLS results can be used to assess the effects of promotion, reenlistment, and accession policies. MOSLS also forecasts the Service's need for newly trained individuals by skill and helps determine the training programs necessary to produce them.

WHERE ELIM AND MOSLS FIT IN CONNECTING RESOURCES TO READINESS

Personnel readiness is part of a hierarchical framework of readiness. Personnel, training, and materiel all factor into unit readiness, which in turn contributes to the readiness of a given Service. That readiness combines with that of other Services—and that of the Joint community—to form overall force readiness.

Our research suggests that a number of *attributes*—for example, number of people qualified and available and their experience level comprise personnel readiness. However, these attributes are removed from resources. The Services do not buy qualified people; rather, they fund *activities* that lead to qualified people. For example, they recruit new enlistees and send them to schools, where they become qualified in a skill. Thus, activities—recruiting, retention, promotion—are what require resources.

Our research further suggests that activities are influenced by things the Services can and cannot control. We call the former *control variables* and the latter *response variables*. Advertising funds is an example of a control variable. The Army can determine how much and what type of advertising it wants to buy. Enlistment is a response variable. The Army attempts to use control variables to influence the response variables. The relevance of ELIM and MOSLS to this discussion is that, in the resource-to-readiness chain, the two models operate in the region between response variables and personnel readiness attributes. Figure S.1 depicts these relationships.

ELIM and MOSLS enter the picture far from the resources. In fact, they do not consider them. What they do consider is the historical performance of response variables, using a combination of modeling techniques including simulation and optimization to predict the ef-

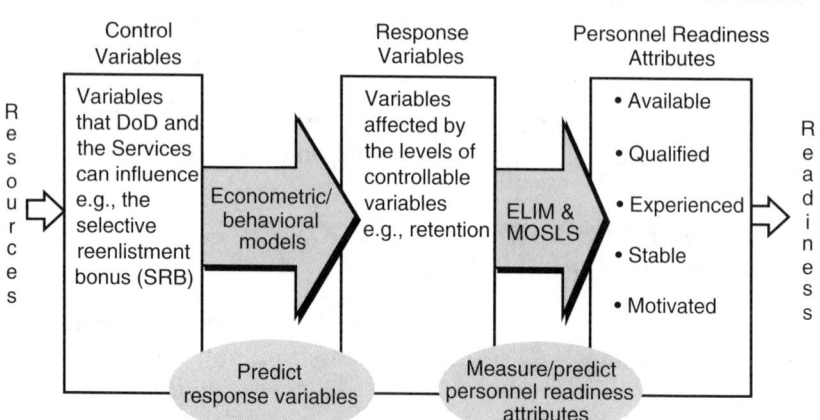

Figure S.1—Where ELIM and MOSLS Fit

fect on the attributes of personnel readiness. The Army then analyzes those predictions and decides if they represent the level of readiness it wants. If not, it can apply its resources differently to improve the prediction. In short, the Army decides what level of readiness it wants and uses ELIM and MOSLS to determine if its current resource allocation will produce it.

However, ELIM and MOSLS make no connection between control and response variables. As Figure S.1 shows, other kinds of models do; those we call econometric or behavioral models. These make predictions about things that are very hard to predict: For instance, how many more and what kinds of people will join the Army if the advertising budget increases by $10 million? Because they attempt to predict human behavior, they are subject to considerable uncertainty. However, they address a key segment of the resources-to-readiness link.

HOW WELL DO ELIM AND MOSLS WORK?

ELIM and MOSLS work well for what they were designed to do. ELIM and MOSLS are useful, and key, tools for Army active enlisted strength management. Both models use analytical techniques that are valid and properly employed, given the original and current uses of the models. The models' short-term predictions are typically accurate. The long-term predictions are also accurate during periods of little change in the Army's structure and policies and in the external variables that influence personal behaviors (e.g., civilian wage and employment rates).

Although ELIM and MOSLS can provide some insight into the connection between resources and readiness, those using them for that purpose must keep the following clearly in mind:

- Neither model directly considers resources.
- The models both make predictions that, in part, hinge on personnel behavior, which is inherently unpredictable.
- Any results are subject to uncertainties the models do not consider. For example, neither model considers variables outside the military—such as civilian unemployment—that can profoundly affect response variables.
- The models may not adequately address interactions among personnel programs. For example, the Army might freeze promotions to obtain short-term savings. But this step may increase losses and drive up recruiting and training costs. The models would predict the former, but not necessarily the latter.

WHAT TO DO?

The Army could improve its ability to assess the effect of resources on readiness if it could link econometric models with ELIM and MOSLS. This is not to say that the link must be electronic. The linking could be procedural. But because the two types of models operate at different points on the resource-to-readiness spectrum, both outputs need to be considered.

Personnel readiness is still only a portion of the spectrum. The task of managing the resource-to-readiness process at the level of unit, Service, and force readiness remains. In theory at least, this task is possible. It would require additional research to identify models and procedures.

ACKNOWLEDGMENTS

We gratefully acknowledge the indispensable assistance we received from Mr. Frank Watrous and CPT Douglas Hersh of the Military Strength Programs Division in the Office of the Army Deputy Chief of Staff for Personnel, both of whom generously gave of their time to ensure we understood the details of the models we studied. We also acknowledge the thoughtful reviews provided by our two RAND colleagues, Sheila Kirby and Herbert Shukiar.

ACRONYMS

AAMMP	Active Army Military Manpower Program
CONUS	Continental United States
C^{4}I	Command, control, communications, computer systems, and intelligence
ELIM	Enlisted Loss Inventory Model
EMF	Enlisted Master File
ETS	Expiration of Term of Service
FELIM	Female version of ELIM
FSA	Force Structure Allowance
GLF	Gain Loss File
IPM	Inventory Projection Model
MOSLS	Military Occupational Specialty Level System
MRC	Major Regional Contingency
MWR	Morale, Welfare, and Recreation
NPS	Nonprior Service
OOTW	Operation Other Than War
OPALS	Officer Projection Aggregate Level System
OSD	Operating Strength Deviation or Office of the Secretary of Defense
PAM	Personnel Authorization Module
POM	Program Objective Memorandum
PS	Prior Service
SORTS	Status of Resources and Training System
SRB	Selective Reenlistment Bonus
TTHS	Trainees, Transients, Holdees, and Students
YOS	Year of Service

Chapter One
INTRODUCTION

BACKGROUND

The breakup of the Soviet Union and the end of the Cold War profoundly affected the military forces of the United States. The "peace dividend" decreased both the force structure and the budget. Both the active and reserve components were reduced, as were the number of troops deployed outside of the continental United States (CONUS). Our national strategic objectives, and the military policies and plans that support those objectives, changed dramatically. The new military strategy placed a greater reliance on strategic mobility to project capable forces where needed throughout the world.

The nature of the demands for military forces has also changed. Although the focus is still on successfully conducting two Major Regional Contingencies (MRCs), the U.S. military has become involved in an increasing number of missions typically characterized as Operations Other Than War (OOTW). The combination of these factors has contributed to concern over the readiness of our military forces.[1] To avoid a "hollow force," questions are being posed about

---

[1] "[W]e have made people and readiness our top priorities." William J. Perry, *Annual Report to the President and the Congress*, February 1995, p. iii. The numerous research efforts and investigative groups addressing various concepts of readiness is one measure of the interest in readiness issues. At RAND, there have been a number of readiness-oriented studies in the Army's Arroyo Center, Project AIR FORCE, and the National Defense Research Institute. The bibliography provides a list of recent studies published on various aspects of readiness.

the level and distribution of resources across various military Services and activities.

The connection between resources and readiness has always proven difficult to quantify. Part of the problem is the complexity of the concept of "readiness." Various definitions of the term have been offered, and the term itself is used for a variety of purposes and at various levels of the military hierarchy. For example, the terms personnel readiness, materiel readiness, unit readiness, joint readiness, and force readiness have all been discussed and analyzed in recent years.

Complicating the problem is the fact that the relationship between resources and readiness is not direct. Resources buy "things," but those "things" do not constitute readiness. They are inputs to readiness that must be combined to produce a combat-oriented output measure that could answer the question, "Ready to do what?" In addition, readiness has a time dimension. If there is a desire to increase readiness, decisionmakers must know not only how much such an increase would cost, but also how long it would take to attain it.

People form a major element of the military force structure, and personnel costs are the largest component of the defense budget. To attract and manage their personnel successfully, the Services allocate various resources to a range of activities. To assist in this allocation, they use a variety of models. From a resource-to-readiness perspective, important questions include how these models work, how well they work, and how useful they are for making the connection between resources and readiness.

This report documents research on how current models can help in understanding the relationship between resources and personnel readiness. It describes two models, ELIM and MOSLS, used by the Army to manage its personnel strength and suggests where these models "fit" in the relationship between resources and readiness.[2]

---

[2] The Enlisted Loss Inventory Model (ELIM), formerly call ELIM-COMPLIP, is used by the Army to manage its enlisted personnel strength at the aggregate level. The Military Occupational Specialty Level System (MOSLS) manages enlisted strength at the grade and MOS level of detail.

The research augments and complements a prior effort examining a similar question for materiel readiness.

PROJECT OBJECTIVE AND APPROACH

The objective of the research was to understand how current models might be used to predict and measure personnel readiness. Four tasks were undertaken to accomplish this objective:

1. Develop a framework for describing and measuring personnel readiness.
2. Identify the various personnel models used by the Services and the Office of the Secretary of Defense (OSD).
3. Describe in detail how and how well a selected subset of these models work.
4. Assess the feasibility of using these models to help predict and measure personnel readiness.

We reviewed the substantial literature on readiness, personnel activities, and the models used to help manage those activities. We also interviewed a wide range of people in various personnel-oriented organizations of the Services and OSD, soliciting their views on personnel readiness and their expertise on the models of interest. The framework we present for examining the relationship between resources and personnel readiness synthesizes various aspects of this wide body of research and the knowledgeable opinions of Service and OSD personnel managers.

OUTLINE

Chapter Two provides a framework for personnel readiness, including a description of the attributes that define it and the activities that contribute to those attributes. The chapter also lists the various models used by OSD and the Services to help manage personnel activities. Chapter Three reviews the U.S. Army strength management process and how the two most important models, ELIM and MOSLS, are used in that process. Chapter Four provides an overview of ELIM and MOSLS, including a listing of the inputs, outputs, and processing approaches. Chapter Five describes where these two models fit in the personnel readiness framework and how they can help in understanding the relationship between resources and personnel readiness. Two appendices provide more detailed descriptions of ELIM and MOSLS.

Chapter Two
A FRAMEWORK FOR PERSONNEL READINESS

This chapter presents a framework for measuring and evaluating personnel readiness and for examining the relationship between resources and personnel readiness. We start by placing personnel readiness in an overall hierarchy of readiness inputs and outputs. We then define the attributes that contribute to its measurement and prediction. We next describe how these attributes are affected by various OSD and Service activities. It is these activities that require resources. We conclude the chapter with an initial list of the various models used by the Services and OSD to manage their personnel activities.

PERSONNEL READINESS IS AN INPUT TO OVERALL FORCE READINESS

Numerous research efforts, many in recent years, have examined various aspects of readiness. A common thread in much of this research is that readiness is not a simple concept that is easily defined and measured.[1] Most attempts at defining readiness focus on the capability of a military force, or on the ability of that force to accomplish specified missions and goals.

Readiness is often described as an output measure; that is, readiness is a capability that results from various personnel, equipment, train-

---

[1] A very good discussion of definitions of readiness is contained in Richard K. Betts, *Military Readiness: Concepts, Choices, Consequences*, Brookings Institution, Washington, D.C., 1995.

ing, mobility, and other inputs.[2] It is also typically easier, because of the difficulty in defining and understanding the concept of readiness, to address readiness issues by focusing on the various "pieces" that make up readiness. This input/output relationship, when viewed in the context of what composes a military force, suggests that there is a hierarchy of readiness "levels" where one level of the hierarchy provides the inputs to the next higher level. Personnel readiness is at the bottom of this hierarchy. It is one of the basic inputs that feeds the overall readiness of the force. Figure 2.1 depicts this hierarchy.

At the top of the hierarchy is the readiness of the force or the ability of the overall force to perform a given mission successfully. A force is composed of units from the active and reserve components of the

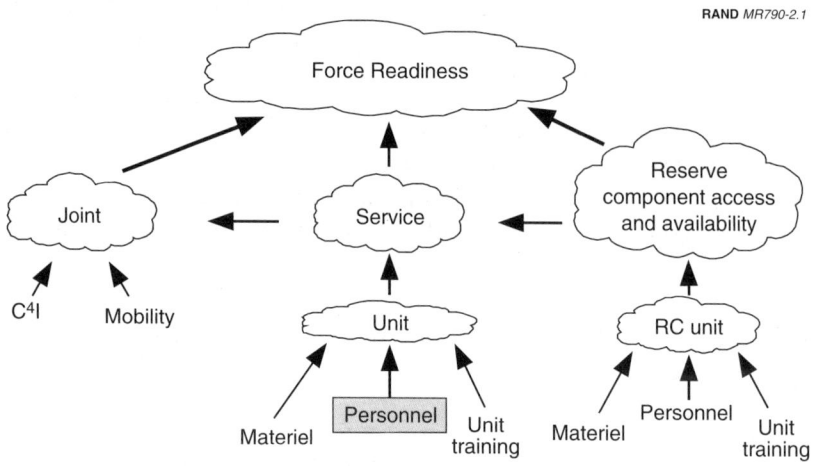

Figure 2.1—Readiness Hierarchy

_____

[2]The Status of Resources and Training System (SORTS) is the joint system used by all the Services to measure the readiness of their units. One common criticism of SORTS is that it measures inputs, not outputs.

various military Services.[3] Therefore, the Service readiness levels for their active and reserve component units are inputs for determining the readiness of the force.

But a force is also composed of joint capabilities, many of which are provided by units of the individual Services. For example, strategic mobility is considered a joint capability but is provided by units, personnel, and equipment of the Army, Navy, and Air Force. The joint world also contributes infrastructure and command, control, communications, computer systems, and intelligence (C^4I) capabilities. As with the Services, the readiness measures for these joint capabilities serve as inputs to determining the readiness of the overall force.

A military Service is composed of a collection of units. The readiness of the separate units can be combined into an overall readiness measure for the Service. The distinction between unit and Service readiness is important because a Service can, and often will, cross-level people and equipment to increase the readiness of specific units. It is possible that two "less ready" units can be "combined" to make one "more ready" unit and one "less ready" unit.[4] Therefore, the readiness of individual units is an input to determining the overall readiness of a Service.

Because SORTS is the widely used measure of military readiness, readiness issues are typically addressed at the unit level. SORTS produces unit "C-levels" that characterize the proportion of the wartime mission the unit can perform.[5] Separate ratings for personnel, materiel, and unit training combine to form an overall unit rating. Therefore, personnel readiness is one component (or input), along

---

[3]Services measure readiness for both active component (AC) and reserve component (RC) units. Since Services may have different resourcing and readiness policies and procedures for their components, it is often useful when thinking about resources-to-readiness issues to keep AC unit readiness separate from RC unit readiness. However, addressing and integrating RC readiness issues are necessary for understanding overall force readiness.

[4]See, for example, Bruce Orvis, H. J. Shukiar, Laurie McDonald, M. G. Mattock, M. R. Kilburn, and M. G. Shanley, *Ensuring Personnel Readiness in the Army Reserve Components*, RAND, MR-659-A, 1996. Section 2 of this document examines the cross-leveling in reserve component units mobilized for Operation Desert Shield/Storm.

[5]A good description of the use of SORTS to report unit readiness is contained in S. Craig Moore, J. A. Stockfish, M. S. Goldberg, S. M. Holroyd, and G. G. Hildebrandt, *Measuring Military Readiness and Sustainability*, RAND, R-3842-DAG, 1991, pp. 10–17.

with materiel readiness and unit training, in determining the overall readiness of a unit.

Thus, personnel readiness is a fundamental input to unit and, by extension, overall readiness. But personnel readiness receives its own inputs, and questions remain about what these are and how to measure them. Other questions pertain to the factors that affect the personnel readiness measures. We discuss these issues next.

CERTAIN ATTRIBUTES DEFINE PERSONNEL READINESS

Our research focuses on the personnel component of unit readiness. Personnel readiness refers to more than the status of an individual. It represents the collective capability of all the individuals assigned to the unit.

Our research suggests that personnel readiness has five attributes. SORTS measures three of them: the percentage of required unit personnel available to deploy, the percentage of unit personnel qualified in their duty skill, and the experience level of the unit measured by the percentage fill of senior grades. Putting aside the positive and negative aspects of SORTS, most would agree that these measures are important for understanding personnel readiness. Therefore, *available, qualified,* and *experienced* are three personnel attributes that contribute to the readiness of both the unit and the Service.

Requirements, or goals, for these attributes are defined by the Services in unit manning documents. These documents specify the numbers of people by skill and grade that are required to perform the unit's wartime mission. Although exact relationships between the attributes and unit readiness are not easily defined, the general view is "the more, the better," and the closer a unit's actual manning comes to the stated goals, the more ready the unit is to perform its mission (or perform it at a higher level).

We believe two other attributes are also important for measuring unit and Service readiness. One is the *stability* of unit personnel; the other is the *motivation* of unit personnel, a measure that has received significant attention in recent years. Stability has much in common with experience, but has a different focus. Where experience relates to the longevity of the force, stability relates to a minimization of the turbulence of the personnel in the force. Experienced people have been in the force for some time; stable people have been in their unit and in the same skill position for some time. The advantage of experienced personnel can be offset by low stability.

Recently, the Services and OSD have become concerned with, and have allocated resources to, the motivation or emotional well-being of military personnel. Senior leaders would like the commitment, morale, and overall "taste" for the military life to be high among their personnel. This desire reflects the recognition that unit readiness can suffer if unit personnel are not motivated to provide the effort needed to use their skills and knowledge effectively.

While quantitative measures of the attributes of availability, qualification, experience, and stability are attainable, there is no obvious objective measure of an individual's motivation or of its unit counterpart, morale or esprit de corps.[6] Motivation is intangible, and the same set of "conditions" can result in different motivation levels for different people. Conditions that affect motivation typically fall under morale, welfare, and recreation or "quality of life" issues and include both individual (e.g., compensation) and family (e.g., housing) concerns. The health of individuals, the health care provided, housing options and conditions, and the availability and cost of child care are just some of the major contributors to motivation.

To summarize briefly, our research suggests that five attributes— available, qualified, experienced, stable, and motivated—are necessary and sufficient for measuring and predicting personnel readiness. These attributes are inputs for determining unit readiness. However, these five attributes themselves are influenced by inputs. The inputs to attributes are the Service and OSD activities that begin

---

[6]Our initial survey of models used to manage personnel readiness issues included no models that specifically addressed motivational aspects. This is not to suggest that such models do not exist, only that there are few that are readily available and widely used. This is not unexpected; motivation has been a concern only in the past five to ten years. Motivational issues and the effect of motivation on personnel readiness is a fertile area for analysis, and we expect that more efforts will be devoted to building relationships in this area. See Charlotte H. Campbell et al., *A Model of Family Factors and Individual and Unit Readiness: Literature Review* and Elyse W. Kerce, *Quality of Life in the U.S. Marine Corps.*

the resource-to-readiness chain by demanding resources. We turn to these activities next.

VARIOUS ACTIVITIES AFFECT PERSONNEL READINESS ATTRIBUTES

In many ways, personnel readiness is more difficult to measure and predict than materiel readiness because it depends on the behaviors and choices of individuals. These behaviors and choices are influenced by both Service policies and procedures and by variables external to the military, such as the civilian unemployment and wage rates. Because of the complexity associated with the behaviors of individuals, the Services closely manage such personnel functional activities such as recruiting and retention.

Each of these functional activities has goals that relate to the goals of the personnel readiness attributes. For example, the Services have monthly recruiting objectives for the number and type of new accessions. Likewise, the Services have retention goals for the number and type of personnel to be retained in the force. Promotion and training policies attempt to match the inventory of personnel to the grade and skill objectives specified in unit staffing documents.

Activity goals do not match directly with the attribute goals. Differences arise from at least two sources—the lack of sufficient resources to apply to the activities and the personal choices and behaviors of individuals. Without sufficient resources, the Services may not be able to recruit, retain, train, or promote the desired number of people. And because uncertainty surrounds the choices of individuals, there is no guarantee that, even with sufficient resources, people will join or stay in the military.

Control and Response Variables Intermingle

The Department of Defense (DoD) or the Services can affect a *control variable* directly; an example is the amount of and eligibility requirements for a selective reenlistment bonus (SRB). A *response variable* is influenced by control variables and directly affects personnel readiness attributes; an example is the number in a targeted population that might reenlist.

In our framework, we believe the functional activities have both response variables and control variables. This relationship is shown in Figure 2.2. The response variables are what the activities are trying to achieve. Examples include the number of people, by type, who enlist in a military service and the number of people who decide to stay in the force. The response variables cannot be directly controlled by the Services because of the influence of individual behaviors. The Service personnel activities attempt to match the response variables with their goals. That is, given that the recruiting commands have a target number of accessions, the outcomes of the response variables influence how closely actual accessions will come to the targets.

As mentioned, functional activities cannot directly determine the values for the response variables. They use control variables to influence personal behaviors, which in turn affect the response variables. That is, the personnel activities use the measures the Services can control to shape the measures they cannot. For example, recruiting commands will put more money into advertising (a control variable) in an attempt to increase the number of high-quality accessions (a response variable). In turn, the number and quality mix of accessions will influence the availability of unit personnel (an attribute). The control variables are what require resources.

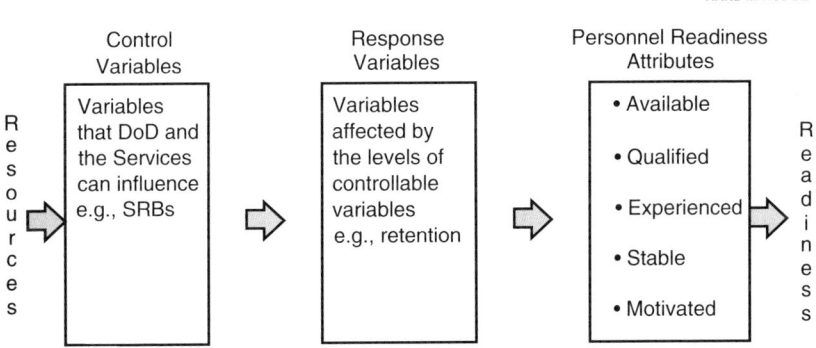

Figure 2.2—The Relationship Between Attributes and Variables

Readiness Metrics

Some readiness-related research efforts that have focused on identifying appropriate readiness measures have produced extensive lists of metrics that relate to readiness. From our perspective, these measures become confusing because they span the control variables, response variables, and attributes of personnel readiness. Figure 2.3 maps one recently proposed set of measures into our framework for personnel readiness.[7]

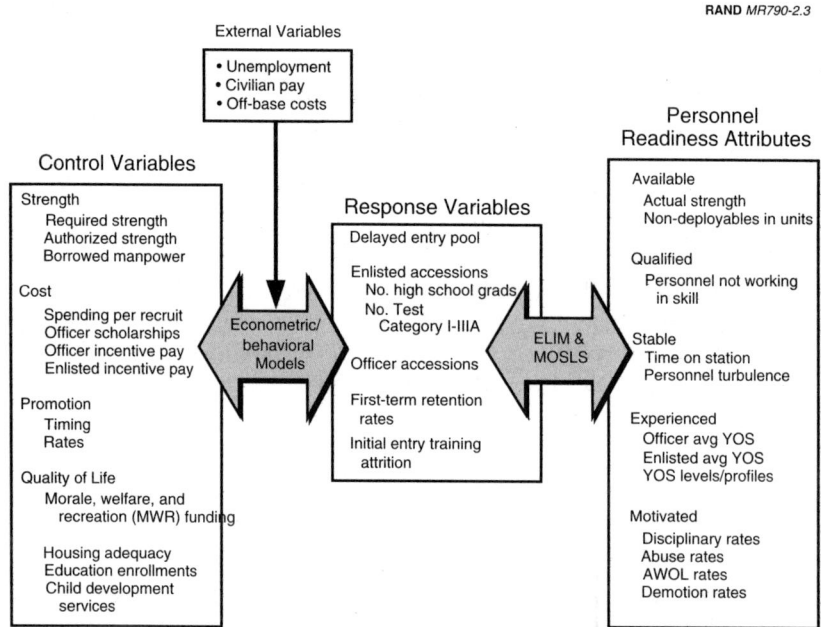

Figure 2.3—Framework for Personnel Readiness

---

[7]These measures are a combination of those proposed by the Logistics Management Institute, a federally funded research and development center, as part of an OSD research project, and subsequent OSD analysis of beneficial readiness measures.

Some useful measures of external variables, control variables, response variables, or attributes are not now included. For example, grade strength and trained (military occupational specialty, MOS) strength seem to be useful measures of the "qualified" attribute. In a similar vein, budgeted grades seem to be a useful control variable as does level of advertising, number of recruiters, level of college fund, amount of enlistment and reenlistment bonuses, end strength, and basic pay. One should assess the *set* of metrics in terms of being complete (no important ones are omitted), unique, and operable (have sufficient definition and meaning).

INITIAL INVENTORY OF PERSONNEL MODELS

The relationships among the control variables, response variables, and personnel readiness attributes are complex and not easily understood. The functional activities use a range of different types of models to help understand these relationships and to decide how many resources of what types are needed to influence the readiness attributes.

The next step in the research was to identify the models used by OSD and the Services to help manage the various functional activities. An initial inventory of these models appears in Table 2.1.

The Services and OSD use models in the personnel functional activities shown in the table columns. Strength management affects the other activities, by providing information or objectives to the recruiting and retention activities that are then used as inputs for their specific models. Strength management also includes promotion and rotation activities, areas in which the Services typically do not use models. Rather, the strength management models develop policies for personnel promotion and rotation. Finally, the comprehensive column includes models that address several functional activities.

This is an initial list because not all available models are identified. Dozens of different models used by Service organizations or contractors address various aspects of personnel management. Some of these models are large, detailed representations of various processes or of personnel behaviors. Other models are small, involving just one or two equations and directed at specific functional areas. During our interviews and literature search, we tried to identify the major

Table 2.1
Initial Inventory of OSD and Service Personnel Models

Organization	Recruiting	Retention	Strength Management	Training	Comprehensive
OSD	Cost performance trade-off model		Forces, Readiness and Manpower Information System		Compensation, Accessions, and Personnel Management Model (CAPM)
Army	FAARRS-SHARE	GRC-SRB Model	ELIM MOSLS OPALS Barron TTHS	Army Training Requirements and Resources System (ATTRS) BLTM	Status Projection System (SPS) Army Flow Model AMCOS
Navy	Production Resource Optimization Model	ACOL Bonus Reenlistment Force Transition Model (B/REFT) Roger	Enlisted Cohort Model (ECO)	Navy Training Reservations System	
Air Force		Career Job Reservation Model (CJR) Bonus Effects Model (BEM)	Total Officer Personnel Projection System (AFTOPPS) Enlisted Force Inventory Projection Model		Related Management Decision Support System (RDSS) Long-Term Readiness Assessment (ULTRA) Sable
Marine Corps	Marine Corps Total Force System		Enlisted Personnel Model OPUS	TRAMS Recruit Distribution Model	

NOTE:
- GRC = General Research Corporation
- ACOL = Annualized Cost of Leaving
- OPUS = Officer Planning Utility System
- FAARRS-SHARE = Forecasting and Allocation of Army Recruiting Resources System–Sequential Hierarchical Allocation of Resource Elements
- BLTM = Battalion-Level Training Model
- TRAMS = Training Management System
- AMCOS = Army Manpower Cost System
- RB = Selective Reenlistment Bonus

models commonly used. The absence of a model in a particular cell in Table 2.1 should not be interpreted to imply that no models exist for that Service in that functional area, only that we did not identify any models in our initial survey. Also, in some cells we may have identified only a subset of the models used by the Services or OSD.

From this list, we made an initial decision to examine the ELIM and MOSLS models used by the Army for strength management. Strength management was chosen as a functional activity since it deals with the whole force and, therefore, has large resource implications. Strength management is also often the focal point for other functional activities. For example, in the Army, ELIM and MOSLS produce recruiting goals and reflect the anticipated outcomes of retention and promotion policies.

The Army was chosen for a number of reasons. It is the largest Service in terms of personnel strength, and its models have a long history of use (and modification).[8]

With this choice for the initial examination of how personnel models work, how well they work, and how they could be useful in the resources-to-readiness relationship, we next turn to an overview of Army strength management and the role ELIM and MOSLS play.

---

[8]In addition, RAND's Arroyo Center had a body of knowledge that could provide initial insights into ELIM and MOSLS.

Chapter Three

ARMY STRENGTH MANAGEMENT

Strength management concerns matching the inventory of people in a military service with the needs for them in units and organizations that accomplish military missions. This chapter describes how the Army manages its strength and uses models to do so. The other Services use a similar generic process, but important specifics could differ by Service.[1]

SPACES

Where does the need for people come from? In general, the *Defense Planning Guidance* tells the Army what missions and scenarios to organize and train for. Internal Army processes lead to decisions about specific types of units to create, whether those units should be reserve or active, and whether those units should be resourced fully or at some lower level. Other processes determine the officer-to-enlisted mix and the grade and skill content for a type of unit.

The result of these force decisions is the Army's *programmed force structure*, which is the set of units and organizations that exists in the current year and that is planned in each future year. The *programmed manpower structure* is the sum of all the requirements for military people by grade and skill in all units and organizations of the

---

[1] For example, at the aggregate level of managing strength the Army uses monthly forecasts as an important dimension. The Air Force includes grades at the aggregate level but only forecasts on an annual basis.

Army programmed force structure.[2] More commonly, this is referred to as the *requirements*. However, budget constraints or policy dictates may limit resourcing of these requirements with budgeted manpower. As a result, a *force structure allowance* is used to define billets in the programmed manpower structure that are planned to be filled in a given time period.[3] These *authorizations* or "spaces" are what strength managers are most concerned with meeting as they deal with personnel management issues.

FACES

How many people by grade and skill are available to fill the spaces? The Army and the Department of Defense request an annual end strength, and the Congress approves (or adjusts it) during the budget process. This end strength needs to be large enough to provide *operating strength* or "faces" against authorizations in the units and organizations as well as to provide for people to be in training or in transition between assignments ("individuals").[4] The level of end strength budgeted and appropriated and how well the Army manages the individuals account and activities such as recruiting, training, and rotation can affect the number of "faces" that can be allocated to the "spaces."

OPERATING STRENGTH DEVIATION

The difference between the number of people available to fill authorizations (operating strength) and the number of authorizations is called the *operating strength deviation* (OSD). If there are more

---

[2]This includes TOE (Table of Organization and Equipment) units and TDA (Table of Distribution and Allowances) units.

[3]DoD policy is that at least 90 percent of requirements will be authorized for fill. Because of past problems in meeting this policy, the National Defense Authorization Act for FY 1996 requires the Secretary of the Army (beginning in 1999) to ensure that officer strength is sufficient to enable the Army to meet at least that percentage of the programmed manpower structure for officers that is provided for in the most recent defense planning. The Secretary of Defense is directed to provide to the Army sufficient personnel and financial resources to meet the requirement.

[4]The TTHS (Trainees, Transients, Holdees, and Students), or "individuals account," is defined as the actual or projected people not filling billets in the programmed manpower structure.

people available than authorizations, the deviation is positive; negative deviation means more spaces than faces. The Army measures operating strength deviation throughout the operating year and as projected into a future year as it represents the capability to provide people to commanders of units who have been led to expect them by virtue of their authorizations. The deviation might be structural (either too many authorizations or not enough operating strength) or frictional (seasonal patterns of personnel entry, loss, and assignments cause differences). Moreover, if authorizations and strength are increasing or decreasing over the year, the balancing of faces and spaces is more difficult. Of course, whether the deviation is positive or negative at any point is influenced by anything that might affect either side of the equation. For example, an overly large force structure, programmed manpower structure, or force structure allowance could lead to a negative deviation, as could insufficient end strength or an overly large individuals account.

Strength managers are usually not responsible for the number of authorizations (although they may forecast future levels) or for the end strength or size of the individuals account (although they may predict future values for the latter given budget estimates of the former). Strength managers are responsible for determining the likely effect of recruiting, promoting, and separating activities on the ability to match faces to spaces, now and in the future. Thus, the objective in managing strength is to minimize the operating strength deviation in the Army, primarily in the enlisted force.[5]

STRENGTH MANAGEMENT IS MODELED BECAUSE OF COMPLEXITY

Strength managers might choose to match current and projected personnel inventory to authorizations in the aggregate, where the focus is on people moving in and out of the Army over time. The following equation reflects this focus:

$$\text{FutureStrength} = \text{CurrentStrength} + \text{Gains} - \text{Losses}$$

---

[5]Officer and warrant officer faces and spaces matter as well. However, the models of interest here deal with the enlisted force and only incorporate officer data to produce comprehensive reports.

The faces and spaces might be also matched on a disaggregate basis, where the match is by skill and grade and the focus is on movement within the Army. A disaggregate equation would be given as

$$\text{FutureTrainedStrength} = \text{CurrentTrainedStrength} + \text{MOSgains} - \text{MOSlosses} + \text{Gradegains} - \text{Gradelosses}$$

All in all, strength management is a complex process with equally complex interactions that benefits from the use of projection models that represent the strength management process. The primary tool of the strength manager is the inventory projection model (IPM), which implements the strength management algorithm with mathematical precision. IPMs come in two varieties, aggregate and disaggregate, corresponding to the two classes of strength management discussed above.

A simple aggregate model might have two dimensions: year of service and term of enlistment (first-term versus career). This is a low-granularity or level-of-detail model; higher-granularity models would have more inventory dimensions, such as grade or a division of the first-term population by accession characteristics (e.g., high/low quality), or the time periods could be in months rather than years. A disaggregate model is very granular (e.g., 300 MOSs). Every increase in granularity adds to model complexity, run time, memory requirements, input detail, and volume of output. For example, in the Army, projections are made over an 84-month time horizon, for some 300 skills, in 9 grades, using 12 personnel quality groups, differentiating male and female, and incorporating policy for recruiting, reclassifying, promoting, and separating. All of these dimensions must be continuously integrated into the future to answer significant questions about readiness and budget.

The first iteration of a model proceeds from the beginning populations (Year 1) to the first projected period (Year 2). Year 2 is entirely determined by Year 1, the rates, and a target strength for Year 2. The process is reiterated, using the same or modified rates, for each additional time period covered by the model. Mathematically, IPMs are Markovian chains.[6] Variations of the algorithms are often possible.

---

[6]The precise Army architecture that implements the inventory projection model will be described in Chapter Four.

For example, gains can become an input, with projected strengths as an output. The Army models can incorporate such variations.

Aggregate models dominate disaggregate models. Because of small cell sizes and other complications, disaggregate models, when summed across all MOSs, produce a less accurate projection of the force than aggregate models. Therefore, many disaggregate models are designed so that the sum of disaggregate strengths and flows can be constrained to the strengths and flows projected by an aggregate model. For example, as will be shown in Chapter Four, ELIM uses historical data to develop aggregate gain and loss projections by month over seven years. These projections become a constraint for MOSLS, which projects how many soldiers will be in each MOS at each grade level in future time periods. The Army thus uses both an aggregate and a disaggregate model. Besides choosing to use an aggregate or disaggregate model, other modeling choices must also be made.

STRENGTH MANAGERS HAVE MODELING CHOICES

Other variations of inventory projection models are possible. Some of the more important distinctions follow:

- **Dynamic versus steady-state:** So far, we have discussed only dynamic IPMs—those that project from one time period to the next. A steady-state model generates the inventory distribution that would result if rates and flows were identical year after year. ELIM and MOSLS are dynamic models.

- **Group versus entity:** So far, we have discussed only group models. Group means that like individuals within the inventories are grouped into cells defined by the dimensions of the model. In an entity model, each individual is separately represented. ELIM and MOSLS are not entity models.

- **Deterministic versus stochastic:** We have been discussing deterministic models (the same inputs produce the same result for every model run). It is possible (and necessary, in the case of entity models) to make the models stochastic, allowing random distributions of outcomes to occur. ELIM and MOSLS are deterministic.

- **Officer versus enlisted:** Because of differences in officer and enlisted personnel management rules, models are almost always specific to either the officer or the enlisted force. ELIM and MOSLS represent the enlisted force.[7]

- **Planning versus programming:** Planning models trade off precision (accuracy, granularity, and input detail) for speed. With a planning model, an action officer might examine a dozen alternative scenarios in an afternoon, working on a PC. A programming model, because of the need for more accuracy, may take a week to set up and all day to run on a mainframe or a work station. ELIM and MOSLS are programming models; ELIM has some limited planning use.

- **Short-term versus long-term:** A short-term model might project monthly from the current month to the end of the current fiscal year (requiring, incidentally, some seasonality of rates). A long-term model would project annually, from the end of one fiscal year to the end of future fiscal years using annualized rates. ELIM and MOSLS have short- and long-term capabilities.

- **Historic versus econometrically adjusted:** The underlying loss model in an IPM is almost always based on rates developed by observing losses in some historic period. In historically adjusted models, these rates are either used "as projected" or are subject to artful manipulation by analysts. In econometrically adjusted models, the rates are either determined or adjusted using forecasts of factors such as unemployment rates or military/civilian wage differences. Coefficients for these factors are developed by regressing historic loss rates on historic series of the factors. ELIM and MOSLS are historically adjusted.

Finally, analysts can choose which operations research techniques to use within the model. Simulation is useful for making predictions. In the short term, an analyst predicts the levels of certain "response" variables, such as strength, assuming that other "control" variables cannot be changed in the short term. For example, the number of new accessions into the training base for the next three months can-

---

[7]For reporting purposes, ELIM results include officer data. Officer strengths are not optimized within ELIM.

not be easily changed, nor can the number of expected losses from the existing force. In the long term, the analyst can set levels for certain control variables such as targeted strength, and then simulate to predict the impact of future behaviors such as retention.

Optimization can be used to answer policy and programming questions. For example, given the loss forecasts, how many new entrants and of which types need to be recruited in certain time periods? The goal is to get the "best" set of policies for accessing, training, promoting, reclassifying, and separating, assuming various constraints on the personnel management system (e.g., the size of the training base or the dollars available to promote people). "Best" is measured against some objective. A typical objective is to minimize the deviation of actual projected strength from targeted authorizations, that is, to minimize the operating strength deviation. The objective function might weigh these deviations by grade, skill, or time period to reflect decisionmaker preferences for penalties.

In this respect, ELIM and MOSLS are somewhat unusual in that they both simulate and optimize. We will examine this characteristic in detail in the next section.

MODELS ARE PART OF A PROCESS

Models do not operate in isolation from the management activities they support. ELIM and MOSLS give personnel managers coherent data for decisionmaking because the outputs of all the separate personnel management activities have been integrated. The two models provide a framework for personnel managers to think about changes in personnel policy that might lead to a lower operating strength deviation. Several generations of Army personnel managers have been imbued with the logic of ELIM and MOSLS, and Army people tend to think through both problems and opportunities in this common framework. Moreover, the models integrate accession, retention, training, promotion, and reclassification policies and organizations by providing an integrated framework for addressing near-term programming adjustments and long-term policy guidance. At least monthly, personnel managers with oversight for the several personnel management activities meet to discuss modeling issues, including policy inputs, policy prescriptions, and projected or predicted model results.

This chapter has reviewed Army strength management, the choices faced in modeling strength management, and the roles that ELIM and MOSLS play. The next chapter discusses how the two models actually work.

Chapter Four
AN OVERVIEW OF ELIM AND MOSLS

This chapter provides an overview of ELIM and MOSLS, two of a family of models used by Army strength managers. It describes the models' general analytic approach, the processing steps involved, and the outputs generated by each. It also discusses the advantages and disadvantages of ELIM and MOSLS for managing the Army's various personnel activities. For a more detailed description of what ELIM and MOSLS do and how they work, see Appendices A and B, respectively.

ELIM OVERVIEW

The Enlisted Loss Inventory Model/Computation of Manpower Program using LInear Programming model, commonly referred to as ELIM, is the primary model used by the Army to manage its enlisted personnel strength at the aggregate level. ELIM was developed during the early 1970s with the principal objective of supporting improved planning and budgeting of the active force and specifying the required monthly draft calls during the drawdown at the end of the Vietnam conflict.[1] It has been extensively modified over the last two decades to capture the evolving objectives, policies, and concerns of the Army strength management community. It has also been modified to take advantage of emerging mathematical programming algo-

---

[1]The General Research Corporation (GRC) originally developed the model and remains the prime contractor for model upgrades and enhancements, in addition to providing overall support to the Army strength management community. It conducts periodic training classes for Army officers new to strength management organizations and maintains documentation on the technical aspects of ELIM.

rithms and technology. Because of the problems that typically surround older models that have been extensively modified, the Army is beginning a multiyear development effort to replace ELIM and to provide an integrating framework to streamline ELIM's interactions with other models and databases.

Figure 4.1 shows how ELIM interacts with other models and data systems. The shaded symbols in the figure reflect data files or calculations that feed ELIM and its primary hard-copy output, the Active Army Military Manpower Program (AAMMP). The unshaded boxes are the other models that interface with ELIM.

ELIM primarily addresses enlisted personnel strength in operating units. However, it tracks and produces output for the total Army end strength, including officers and personnel in the individuals account. Officer strengths are provided by the Officer Projection Aggregate Level System (OPALS). The individuals account includes personnel in various training categories, on medical leave, hospitalized, in criminal detention, or in-transit between duty locations. Individuals account personnel levels are input from the Trainees, Transients, Holdees, and Students (TTHS) model.

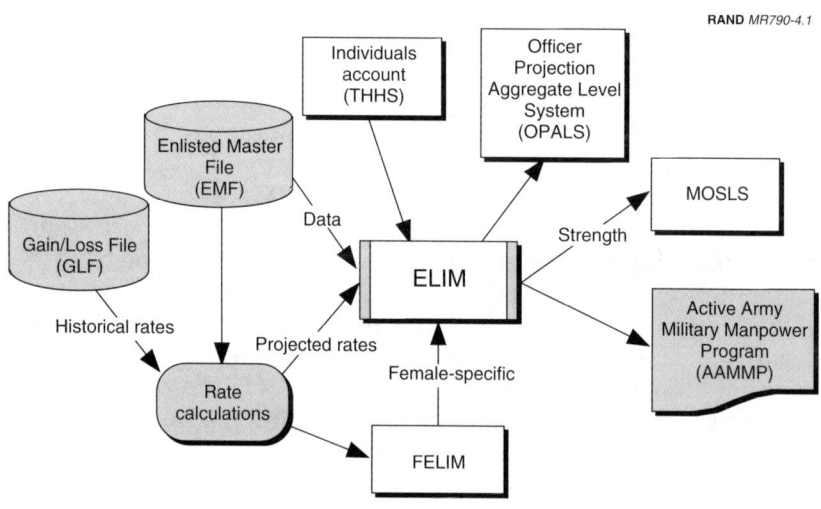

Figure 4.1—Relation of ELIM to Other Models and Databases

The FELIM model is a female-only version of ELIM. It was developed in the late 1970s in response to the increased interest in the accession and management of female enlisted personnel.[2] FELIM is a mirror image of ELIM that produces the female portion of the AAMMP and provides female strength and accession data to ELIM.

ELIM GENERAL ANALYTIC APPROACH AND ARCHITECTURE

The model takes a two-step analytical approach. First, a simulation forecasts future enlisted personnel levels, starting with the current enlisted inventory and estimating, based on historical data, monthly losses for seven years into the future. In the second step, a mathematical programming optimization routine determines the monthly accession levels needed to minimize the operating strength deviation (the difference between "faces" and "spaces") given various constraints that exist in the personnel management system. The overall model architecture is shown in Figure 4.2.

In simplest terms, ELIM determines the number of annual accessions needed during each of the seven inventory projection years. It determines these accessions after applying losses and comparing the remaining enlisted force with required end strength. Three things complicate this process. First, ELIM projects on a monthly basis. Second, accessions are broken down into eight characteristic groups (see Table A.1 for the makeup of these groups) and constraints are imposed on the composition of the accessions in these groups (e.g., number in a given mental category). Finally, within a year, seasonal constraints can be imposed on the monthly availability of a given characteristic group's accessions. For example, a composition constraint used during a recent analysis required that 67 percent of each year's accessions come from male high school graduates in mental category I-IIIA. A seasonal constraint might require a percentage of those accessions to come in July.

---

[2]FELIM was developed because ELIM, constrained by its original design and processing capabilities, could not accommodate the increased number of variables resulting from distinguishing males and females. One of the objectives of the current model development and enhancement is to combine males and females into a single model.

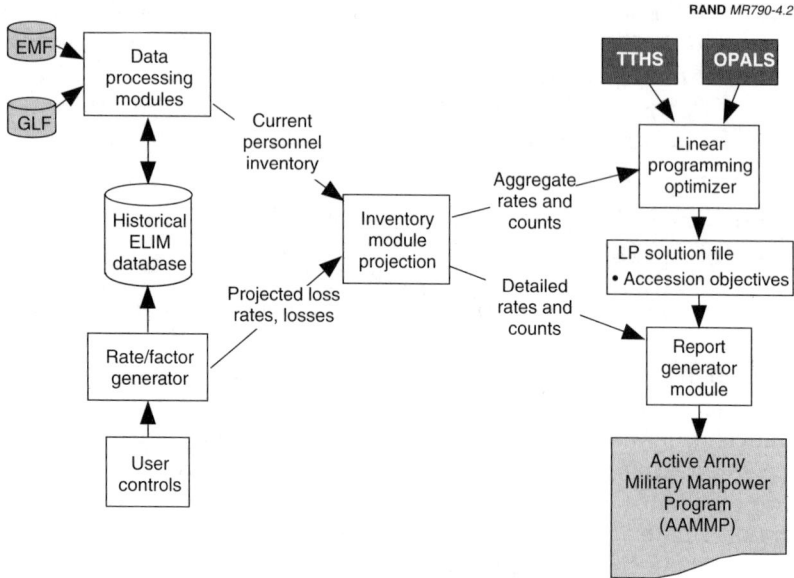

Figure 4.2—ELIM Architecture

The objective of the inventory projection is to determine the number of accessions needed to minimize the monthly operating strength deviation while conforming to all composition and seasonal constraints. No month carries more weight than any other month, and the optimal number of accessions over the 84-month period may lead to positive or negative deviations in specific months. Constraints can be imposed to ensure that these deviations remain within acceptable bounds.

On a more detailed level, here's how ELIM works. The modeling process involves the following four steps:

1. Prepare model inputs.
2. Project enlisted inventory.
3. Determine optimal accession levels.
4. Produce model output.

In the short term, the simulation projects the expected outcomes of events that have occurred in previous time periods. For example, the simulation "knows" how many soldiers will reach the end of their current enlistment contract (ETS) in each future month (and the expected number who will reenlist or extend at that point and for every month prior to that point). The simulation also has access to the future output of training pipelines. Therefore, the short-term inventory predictions are largely "fixed" by past decisions and are difficult for the Army to adjust by changing policies or increasing resource levels.

In the next step in the ELIM process, a linear programming model determines the optimal set of enlisted accessions required to meet the operating strength objectives over the seven-year horizon. These accessions are constrained by recruiting objectives for various types of enlisted people (e.g., gender, education or test scores, or seasonal recruiting constraints). The model also balances the population of different groups by tracking the movement of people through the system (e.g., moving first-term enlistees into career status).[3]

Model outputs are used in three general areas. The main hard-copy output of ELIM—the AAMMP—is used by various personnel management organizations to understand the current and future status of enlisted inventory. In this role, the AAMMP is a primary document in the determination of the Program Objective Memorandum (POM) and the budget. ELIM output also provides the monthly accession goals, both by quantity and type of recruit, to the Recruiting Command. Finally, ELIM outputs are input to MOSLS, where they act as aggregate constraints on MOSLS training pipeline projections.

MOSLS OVERVIEW

The Military Occupational Specialty Level System, or MOSLS, is the model used by ODCSPER and PERSCOM to balance the MOS and grade-level requirements of the Army with the available population.

---

[3] The model can also use entry-level training base capacity and budget constraints for the total force. These capabilities are not currently used.

It complements ELIM in that it provides grade and MOS detail, which ELIM does not consider.[4]

MOSLS supports enlisted personnel policy at two levels. At the most aggregate level, MOSLS enables Army analysts to explore the implications of policies and behaviors that affect the Service's need for total numbers of individuals of certain skills and grades. MOSLS also supports the analysis of voluntary loss behavior and of involuntary loss policies upon the entire enlisted force. At the more detailed MOS and grade level, MOSLS results can be used to assess the effects of promotion, reenlistment, and accession policies. MOSLS also forecasts the Service's need for newly trained individuals by skill and helps determine the training programs necessary to produce such individuals.

MOSLS is one system within the Army's strength management family of models, resources, and products. Figure 4.3 shows how MOSLS interacts with ELIM, other models, and data systems.

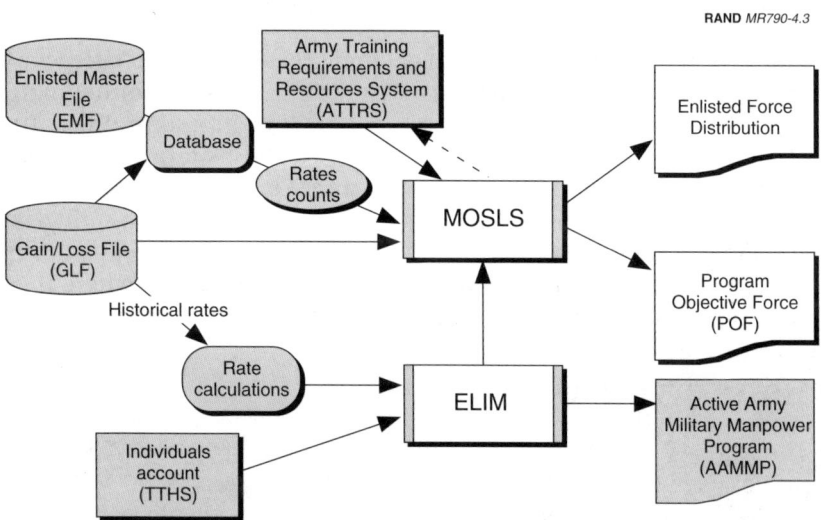

Figure 4.3—Relation of MOSLS to Other Models and Databases

---

[4]The modification to ELIM will include the grade dimension.

MOSLS GENERAL ANALYTIC APPROACH AND ARCHITECTURE

Like ELIM, MOSLS uses both optimization and simulation to consider the ways the personnel community can control the enlisted force, the constraints upon various management options, and events beyond the control of the Service. The optimization function prescribes the best set of personnel management actions for what the Army can control—promotion, reclassification, training load, and forced losses. The optimization models consider legal, resource, and budget constraints when determining the best sets of policies.

The simulation models predict the behavior of the force beyond the Army's control. Simulation provides a more accurate representation of the future force by replicating probable loss, aging patterns, and training graduation rates, which management policies cannot directly alter.

MOSLS has three primary elements: the pre-processor module and its inputs, the trained strength model, and the post-processor module. Figure 4.4 provides a schematic of the architecture and how its components relate to each other. In general, the pre-processor determines the targets to which the model should optimize and the constraints that limit the optimization. It also includes the training simulation model, which projects how many individuals will be graduating from each skill training course.

The trained strength model is a large network model that uses the trained output of the training simulation model and the targets and

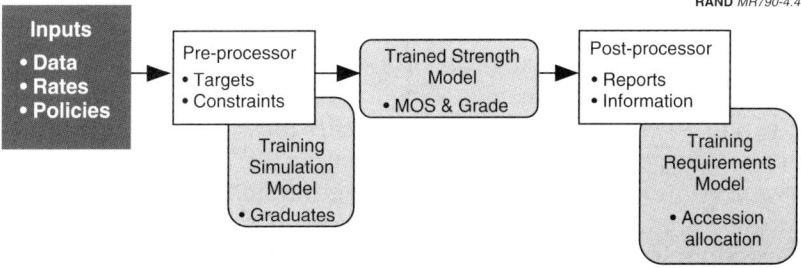

Figure 4.4—MOSLS Architecture

constraints of the pre-processor to model the most optimal force achievable.

The post-processor includes the training requirements model, which considers the optimal force output from the trained strength model and reconsiders how the training simulation model should have allocated individuals across skill training course. The post-processor also compiles various output reports from MOSLS. The key outputs of MOSLS are the Enlisted Force Distribution and the Program Objective Force.

As Figure 4.4 indicates, MOSLS contains three models: the training simulation model (in the pre-processor module), the trained strength model, and the training requirements model (in the post-processor module). The training simulation model makes an initial estimate of the output of the MOS training pipeline over the 84 months of inventory projection. The second model, the trained strength model, then takes the forecast of the training simulation model and combines it with promotions, reclassifications, and losses to produce a detailed inventory projection, which it then manipulates to minimize differences between MOS inventory and requirements by adjusting promotions, reclassifications, and forced losses. This process iterates until the MOS differences show no improvement between iterations. The training requirements model then picks up, taking the results of the trained strength model and determining what input is necessary to the training pipeline to meet the detailed force structure requirements.

SUMMARY

ELIM and MOSLS are key tools for Army active enlisted strength management. The main advantage of ELIM and MOSLS is that they integrate several personnel functional activities. By relating recruiting, training, and retention at the aggregate level, ELIM provides an organized process for addressing strength management issues. By integrating training, promotion, retention, and reclassification at a disaggregrated level, MOSLS provides an organized process for trained strength management, with detailed monthly updates to refine prior forecasts and observe the consequences of enlisted trained strength management policies.

ELIM and MOSLS both use analytical techniques that are valid and properly employed, given the original and current uses of the models. The models' short-term predictions are typically very accurate. The long-term predictions are also accurate during periods of little change in the Army's structure and policies, and in the external variables that affect personal behaviors (e.g., civilian wage and employment rates). Monthly updates and discussions that accompany the updates help adjust the models' predictions and refine prior forecasts by incorporating changes in the Army environment or in other assumptions.

However, it is important to remember that ELIM's optimization module and MOSLS' simulation and optimization modules specify the policies necessary to achieve the specified future force structure goals. Predictions of future values hinge on the assumption that planned policy changes will be implemented, and that unforeseen events or policy changes will not affect the enlisted force. If unexpected policy changes occur or if the policy decisions prescribed by prior ELIM and MOSLS runs are not implemented, then the models' future predictions will vary from actual events.

ELIM and MOSLS also have a number of limitations. Neither model can be considered "user-friendly" because of the complexity of the models and long run times required. Because ELIM was built over two decades ago and has been substantially modified over time, it is fairly opaque, making it difficult to understand. The Army's multiyear effort to develop a replacement for ELIM should correct this limitation.

ELIM is also fairly complex as a result of the numerous data groupings and rates that are used to transition these groups into, through, and out of the personnel system. It was built and is used primarily for programming purposes. It can be, and has been, used for planning studies, but its complexity and lack of transparency hinder an analyst's ability to do "what-if" types of analyses. Although it provides a quicker turnaround than other models such as MOSLS, it still takes two hours or longer for an ELIM run. Again, the use of more modern software and algorithmic procedures should help to shorten the run times.

MOSLS also has a long run time and requires familiarity with the model operations to conduct the monthly runs. What-if excursions are not a practical use of MOSLS, and it is unlikely that the Army will ever be able to conduct the monthly MOSLS runs independent of the civilian contractor. The MOSLS results are well documented and available in numerous data reports. However, the reports themselves are not always easily understandable, and the model processes that contribute to the results are opaque and require considerable expertise to explain. Again, the Army will probably not be able to sustain an internal expertise. The extraordinary number of calculations that complicate MOSLS, however, provide the level of detail that is so helpful to Army strength management.

An additional limitation of ELIM is the sensitivity of its predictions and the impact this has on budgets. Strength management addresses large-magnitude policies and programs. The active end strength includes approximately half a million soldiers with a military personnel budget of approximately $20 billion. Although ELIM is fairly accurate in its predictions, especially in the short term, a small percentage over or under estimate can result in a several hundred million dollar difference between the estimated and actual military personnel budget.

Finally, ELIM and MOSLS are but two parts of an overall process. These models can help understand how best to achieve future goals, but the whole process depends on when and how policies are changed or implemented and on how the propensities of people to enter or stay in the Army change.

Chapter Five
USING ELIM AND MOSLS TO RELATE RESOURCES TO PERSONNEL READINESS

In the previous chapters, we presented a framework for relating resources to personnel readiness and described how two models, ELIM and MOSLS, are used by the Army to manage enlisted personnel strength. In this chapter we address two remaining issues—where ELIM and MOSLS (and other similar models) "fit" in the resources-to-personnel-readiness framework, and how the Army and OSD can use these models to examine the relationship between resources and personnel readiness.

PLACING ELIM AND MOSLS IN THE PERSONNEL READINESS FRAMEWORK

ELIM and MOSLS use historical data to forecast future personnel gains and losses and, when combined with projections of the current inventory, estimate the number of enlisted personnel at both the aggregate and disaggregate (grade and skill) levels. Therefore, ELIM and MOSLS (and similar models) relate anticipated values of the response variables to current and future measures of the available, qualified, and experience attributes.

The other link in the resources-to-personnel-readiness framework is filled by models that address personal behaviors and the variables that influence those behaviors. These econometric, or behavioral, models relate the control variables to the response variables. They predict values for the response variables given decisions on the distribution of resources across the control variables. Figure 5.1 shows the placement of ELIM and MOSLS and the behavioral models in our resources-to-personnel-readiness framework.

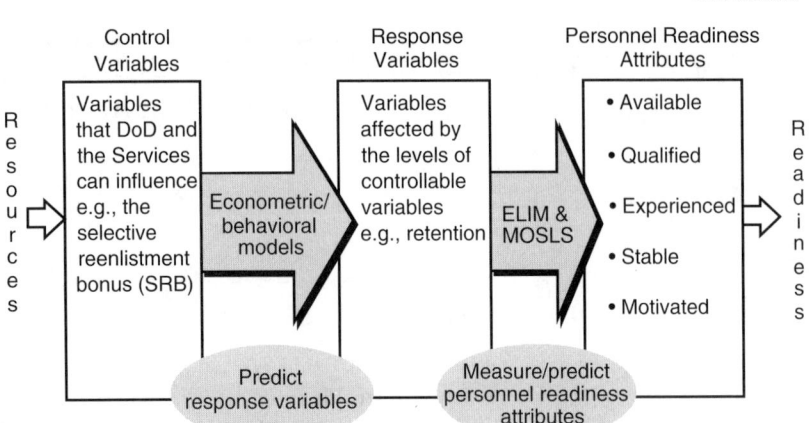

Figure 5.1—Where ELIM and MOSLS Fit

In this "forward" direction, the models are primarily used to understand near-term personnel readiness issues. That is, given the current and planned distribution of resources and the personnel responses that are expected to result from those resource decisions, ELIM and MOSLS estimate the current and near-term values for the personnel readiness attributes. This is the primary role of the simulation portions of ELIM and MOSLS.

Longer-term personnel readiness issues are addressed by using the models in the reverse direction. The optimization portions of ELIM and MOSLS prescribe the goals for the response variables (e.g., the number of new recruits that are needed) given the targets for the personnel readiness attributes (e.g., the desired future operating strength). The behavioral models use the prescribed goals of the response variables to estimate the required resource distribution across the control variables (e.g., the number of recruiters or advertising dollars). This "backward" use of the models is shown in Figure 5.2.

We do not mean to imply that the behavioral models interface with ELIM and MOSLS; they do not. These models must be connected by people within the organizations who deal with the two links in the connection between resources and personnel readiness. The

Using ELIM and MOSLS to Relate Resources to Personnel Readiness   37

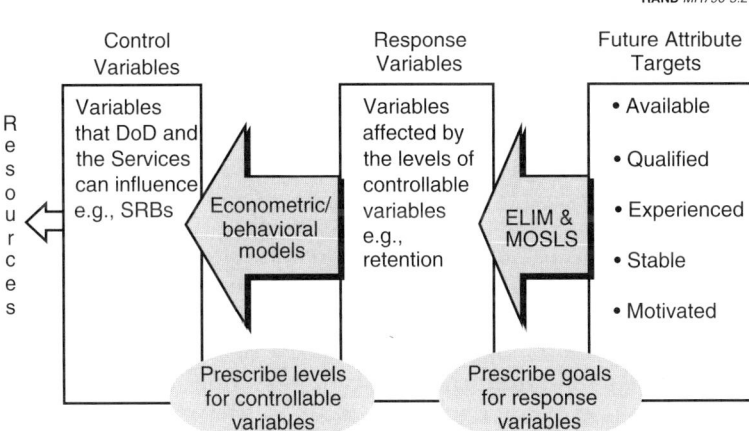

Figure 5.2—ELIM and MOSLS Work in Both Directions

strength management organizations must convey outputs of ELIM and MOSLS to the recruiting, retention, and training organizations. These organizations then craft the appropriate inputs to the behavioral models. Likewise, the recruiting, retention, and training organizations must pass to the strength management organizations the anticipated values of the response variables based on the results of their behavioral models. The gain, loss, and training rates can then be adjusted for input to ELIM and MOSLS. The connection between resources and personnel readiness depends on this information being communicated in a timely and accurate fashion.

PLACING ELIM AND MOSLS IN THE READINESS HIERARCHY

In our hierarchy of readiness levels, ELIM and MOSLS estimate certain personnel readiness attributes at the Service, not unit, level. The models address the total Army enlisted strength, not the attributes of the specific personnel assigned to units. Assumptions about the distribution of personnel to units are needed to estimate the personnel readiness attributes at the unit level.

There are intervening personnel management and decision systems between personnel readiness as measured by the attributes at the Service level and a unit's ability to deploy and employ. The Army's personnel management distribution system strives to place the right soldier in the right job at the right time. But the connection between measures of the Servicewide personnel attributes and unit personnel readiness can be masked for several reasons.

The Army headquarters, major commands, and local commanders all set priorities for assigning personnel to units or for filling specific slots within a unit. The Army's "tiered readiness" concept sets higher priorities, and therefore, higher personnel levels, to selected units in the force. Rather than uniformly allocate personnel to units, some units are manned at 100 percent (or even more than 100 percent) of required strength. Others, lower in the priority scheme, will have a lower percentage of their personnel positions filled.

Other factors play a role in the assignment of soldiers to specific units. Decisions and judgments are made at every level in the personnel assignment process. The need to train a soldier en route to a new assignment, the requirement for hardship or other types of delays in reporting to a unit, and even inaccurate data about unit personnel needs can all lead to problems in matching trained people to unit needs in a timely fashion. Moving hundreds of thousands of people annually among thousands of units and hundreds of locations generates a certain amount of friction. Thus, even if the Army had sufficient available and qualified soldiers Servicewide, their presence in the right units is not ensured. And if mistakes are made or priorities change, it is traumatic to individuals and to the Army itself to "right" things by constantly shifting people among units.

Time is an element of the process as well. Understanding readiness is, at least in part, understanding the time required to move a force from a current level of capability to a desired one. For anticipated missions, a force can provide the needed capability immediately. For unanticipated missions, the force needs time to get ready—time to acquire and train personnel, buy or repair equipment and supplies, and assemble and move to the specified location. Much of current interest in the relationship between resources and readiness revolves around understanding how many and what types of resources are necessary to have the force ready for the less demanding anticipated missions while providing a sufficient base to be able to expand quickly enough to meet more demanding unanticipated missions. ELIM and MOSLS estimate the time needed to increase end strength or to train more personnel. Therefore, they can be useful tools for understanding how long it would take to achieve higher personnel readiness levels.

CAUTIONS ABOUT USING ELIM AND MOSLS TO RELATE RESOURCES TO PERSONNEL READINESS

ELIM, MOSLS, and other personnel-related models are helpful for understanding the relationship between resources and personnel readiness. ELIM and MOSLS provide estimates of the current and future levels of available, qualified, and experienced personnel in the force, and they can inform decisionmakers of the time needed to achieve different levels for these variables. However, four sources of uncertainty must be recognized when attempting to connect resources to readiness: the inherent uncertainty when predicting behavior, inadequately capturing the relationship among different program objectives, the model's assumption that prescribed policies will be carried out and the uncertain effect of time.

First, predicting personal behaviors is complex and the subject of an extensive body of research that attempts to model the relationship between various factors and a person's propensity to enlist or reenlist in the military. Some of these factors are external to the military itself; for example, civilian unemployment rates and the relationship between civilian and military pay rates are typical variables in many behavioral models. But future levels of these external variables may be difficult to quantify, adding uncertainty to the behavioral models' estimates of the response variables. This uncertainty influences the expected gain and loss rates used by ELIM and MOSLS, which adds uncertainty to the estimates of the number of available, qualified, and experienced soldiers in the force. In essence, the accuracy of the ELIM and MOSLS estimates is based on the accuracy of the estimates for the response variables.[1]

---

[1] This also, of course, applies to the input data and to the historical data used by ELIM and MOSLS to generate various rates. If these data are inaccurate or not provided in a timely manner, the output of ELIM and MOSLS will reflect the inaccuracies.

Second, uncertainty results because the relationships among different personnel program objectives are complex and may not be adequately captured within the models. Actions in one personnel functional area may have unanticipated effects in others. For example, promotions may be delayed in an attempt to reduce short-term personnel costs. This may, in turn, adversely affect short-term retention, drive up recruiting goals, and decrease the number of trained soldiers in the force. The savings in personnel pay may be more than offset by the increases in recruiting and training costs. ELIM and MOSLS do not directly consider these types of relationships. It is the responsibility of the specific organizations to recognize the indirect effects and tailor ELIM and MOSLS inputs and factors accordingly.

Third, ELIM and MOSLS assume that the policies they prescribe will be followed. The models estimate how many and what types of people should be recruited, how many should be trained in specific skills, and how many should be promoted. If the prescribed policies are not followed or the prescribed goals are not attained, the actual levels of the personnel readiness attributes will differ from those estimated by the models.

Finally, complex and most likely nonlinear relationships exist among policies, resources, and outcomes that mask any easy mapping of resources to personnel readiness attributes, much less to unit readiness or even unit status levels. These relationships make the time it will take to affect a readiness attribute uncertain. Increased resources may not result in increased readiness, or the time needed to have an effect may vary. For example, the Army may allocate additional resources to increase end strength. Initially, the increased end strength will be absorbed by the individuals account because more soldiers will be in the recruiting and training pipelines. The effect is no short-term increase in the units' operating strength and, therefore, no immediate increase in readiness levels. Conversely, the Army may reduce resources by decreasing end strength. Fewer soldiers will be recruited and trained, resulting in a decrease in the individuals account with, potentially, an increase in the operating strength, and readiness, of units. And, of course, resources may not change at all, but personnel readiness attribute levels may, because personnel policy changes affect the number of people available in the individuals and operating accounts.

PERSONNEL READINESS ATTRIBUTE LEVELS AND SORTS MEASURES

The unit status report, which is widely taken as a measure of unit readiness (although it is designed as a measurement of available resources), measures available, qualified, and experienced soldiers on continuous scales at the unit level (e.g., percentage of requirement). However, increases or decreases in the percentages may or may not change the SORTS-related readiness measure for the unit (i.e., C-1, C-2, etc.).[2] That is, the SORTS measures do not always reflect the effect of resource inputs. The impact on the SORTS measures of increased or decreased levels of a unit's personnel readiness attributes depends both on the previous readiness level and whether the change is sufficient to move a unit into a different category level (e.g., from C-2 to C-1 for an increase in attribute levels or from C-2 to C-3 for a decrease). The SORTS category levels are discrete while the individual measures are continuous. As an example, a unit could get "better" or "worse" by nine percentage points and the SORTS measure may not change, because the change was not large enough to bridge a SORTS threshold. Alternatively, a unit could increase or decrease one percentage point and the SORTS measure would change (e.g., move from 89 to 90 percent and thus from C-2 to C-1).

---

[2]The rating thresholds for the various personnel categories are as follows:

Rating	Personnel Area	Percentage
C-1	Total	90
	MOS	85
	Grade	85
C-2	Total	80
	MOS	75
	Grade	75
C-3	Total	70
	MOS	65
	Grade	65
C-4	Total	< 70
	MOS	< 65
	Grade	< 65

The multiple category levels in SORTS may also mask outcomes. For example, a unit might move down a level in one resource category (e.g., number of senior grade personnel) but stay constant in another category (e.g., number of available people) because the distribution system has assigned junior instead of senior people. Overall, the Army may have high levels of available and qualified soldiers, but the maldistribution may skew the individual category scores. The system automatically scores the unit at the lowest category level under the assumption that all categories have equal weights.

Being on the "razor's edge" of readiness is not bad. In fact, it is the most efficient place to operate in terms of perceived relationships between resources and readiness within the SORTS system. For example, if a Service designs its units to be at a C-2 level (has resources to undertake the bulk of wartime missions), the numerical percentage that must be achieved on the SORTS category levels is at least 80 percent. While a unit with 87 percent of its resources may in fact be more ready, in terms of "reported readiness" it is no more ready than a unit that reports 80 percent of its resources are available. Over time and in the aggregate, the incentive is to allocate resources to units to achieve exactly 80 percent and to use the freed-up resources to build more units or to buy more modern equipment.

If a Service could manage perfectly, it has incentives to stay on the razor's edge. However, since a Service cannot manage perfectly, it has to make a choice: Should it provide resources at a level above a desired readiness state and ensure readiness at that desired state but potentially "waste" resources the majority of the time, or should it provide a lower level of resources, realizing it will not attain the desired readiness goals at least part of the time but will "waste" fewer resources? As an example, assume a Service can manage with a 4 percent margin of error and the desired readiness level is C-2 (i.e., 80 percent). It could choose to set category goals of 84 percent, thus ensuring that, even with the worst error, the unit will always be C-2. Or it could choose to set category goals at 82 percent with a savings in resources, accepting that the unit will fall below C-2 approximately half the time. In addition to its overall strategy and approach, how well a Service can forecast, plan, and manage will affect both resources and readiness.

EXTENDING THE RESEARCH

In this report, we have described a framework for relating resources to personnel readiness and showed where and how two specific personnel models fit in that framework. In Figure 2.1, we presented a hierarchy of readiness issues in which the output of one level in the hierarchy became an input for the next higher level. Personnel readiness was a basic input in that hierarchy, an input that helps determine both unit readiness and Service readiness.

Further research is needed to identify, examine, and evaluate the models that may help make the connections among other portions of the readiness hierarchy. For example, personnel readiness is but one input for determining unit, or Service, readiness. Theoretically, a model should be able to combine the personnel readiness attributes with similar attributes for equipment/materiel and collective training to produce measures of unit readiness.

Our hierarchy distinguishes between unit readiness and Service readiness and between the readiness of active and reserve units. Because of cross-leveling (i.e., moving people between units), the overall readiness of a Service is not a simple combination of the readiness of individual units. Theoretically, a model could consider the range of options for combining people and equipment across units to enhance the readiness of specific units. Such a model would help clarify trade-offs between having a subset of units at high readiness levels with other units at low levels versus maintaining a wider range of units at "medium" readiness levels. Such decisions may vary by type of unit or by Service.

Although the readiness modeling efforts concentrate on active component readiness, the readiness levels of reserve units are equally important, especially for the functional capability that resides primarily in the reserve forces. New models should be built or existing ones enhanced to integrate the readiness of RC units with that of AC units. Informed resource decisions that consider the Total Force would then be possible.

Moving up the hierarchy, Service readiness measures combine with joint readiness measures to produce a measure of overall force readiness. Again, theoretically a model should exist that takes the Service and joint readiness inputs and produces a force readiness measure. Such an analytical capability is necessary for determining how best to balance resources among the various elements of force readiness. As an example, units must be ready to deploy, and joint strategic lift assets must be ready to transport those units to the theater of operations. Resources should be balanced so that the readiness of units matches the availability and readiness of the lift assets. The overall system is not performing efficiently if units are waiting at an airport or seaport for lift to arrive or if aircraft or ships are waiting for the units to be ready to embark.

Readiness and the distribution of resources to maximize readiness are important areas for research in the current defense environment. The research described here should contribute to the understanding of the connection between resources and readiness, but it is only a piece of a larger puzzle. Understanding the other pieces requires additional research.

Appendix A
DESCRIPTION OF ELIM

This appendix provides a description of ELIM in and an overview of the model's general analytic approach, architecture, inputs, outputs, and processing steps. It concludes by listing the advantages and disadvantages of ELIM for managing the Army's various personnel activities.

BACKGROUND

The Enlisted Loss Inventory Model, commonly referred to as ELIM, is the primary model the Army uses to manage its enlisted personnel strength at the aggregate level. ELIM was developed during the early 1970s to support improved planning and budgeting of the active force (and specify the required monthly draft calls) during the drawdown in strength at the end of the Vietnam conflict.[1] It has been extensively modified over the past two decades to capture the evolving objectives, policies, and concerns of the Army strength management community. It has also been modified to take advantage of emerging mathematical programming algorithms and technology. Because of the problems that typically surround older models that have been extensively modified, the Army is beginning a multiyear development effort to replace ELIM and to provide an integrating automated framework with other models and databases.

---

[1] The General Research Corporation (GRC) originally developed the model and remains the prime contractor for model upgrades and enhancements, in addition to providing overall support to the Army strength management community. GRC conducts periodic training classes for Army officers new to strength management and maintains documentation on ELIM's technical aspects.

How ELIM interacts with other models and data systems is shown in Figure A.1. The shaded boxes in the figure reflect data files or calculations that feed ELIM and the primary hard-copy output of ELIM, the Active Army Military Manpower Program (AAMMP). The unshaded boxes are other models that interface with ELIM.

ELIM focuses on the enlisted personnel strength in operating units. It also tracks and produces output for the total Army personnel strength, including officers and personnel in the individuals account. Officer strengths are provided by the Officer Projection Aggregate Level System (OPALS). The individuals account includes personnel in training, hospitalization, criminal detention, and in-transit between duty locations. Individuals account personnel levels are input from the Trainees, Transients, Holdees, and Students (TTHS) model.

The FELIM model is a female-only version of ELIM. It was developed in the late 1970s in response to the increased interest in the acces-

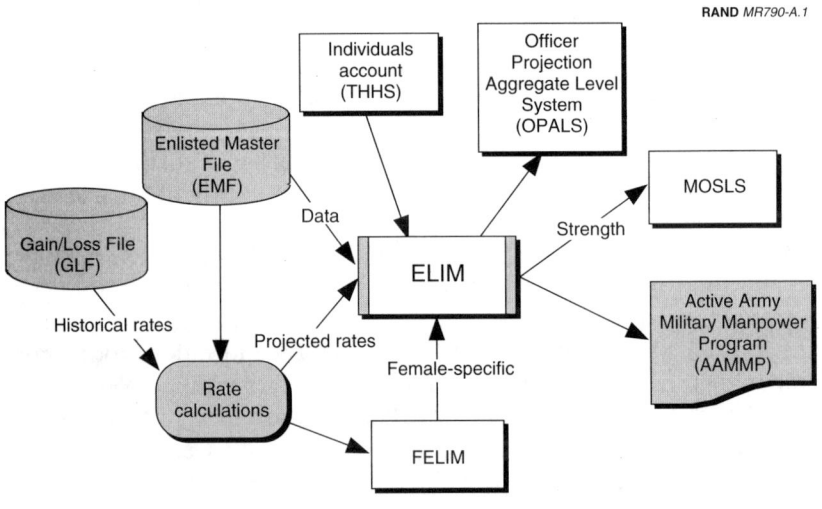

Figure A.1—ELIM Is Key Part of Family of Strength Management Models

sion and management of female enlisted personnel.[2] FELIM, a mirror image of ELIM, produces the female portion of the AAMMP and provides female strength and accession data to ELIM.

GENERAL ANALYTIC APPROACH AND ARCHITECTURE

ELIM takes a two-step analytical approach. First, simulation is used to forecast future enlisted personnel levels for the current year, the budget year, and five years of the Future Years Defense Plan (FYDP). It starts with the current enlisted inventory and estimates, based on historical data, monthly losses for the seven-year period. In the second step, a mathematical programming optimization routine determines the monthly accession levels needed to minimize the operating strength deviation (the difference between "faces" and "spaces") given various constraints in the personnel management system.

The second step, or optimization, is performed in either of two ways depending on the objectives of the particular ELIM run. One method is to fix the total strength and allow the monthly accessions to "float." In this mode, projected losses from the force determine the required monthly accessions. In the alternative approach, the monthly accession levels are fixed and the resulting total strength is allowed to float. Here, the projected losses from the force determine the end strength projections.

In simplest terms, ELIM determines the number of annual accessions needed during each of the seven inventory projection years. It determines these accessions after applying losses and comparing the remaining enlisted force with required end strength. Three things complicate this process. First, ELIM projects on a monthly basis. Second, accessions are broken down into eight characteristic groups (see Table A.1 for the makeup of these groups) and constraints are imposed on the composition of the accessions in these groups (e.g., number in a given mental category). Finally, within a year, seasonal

---

[2]FELIM was developed because ELIM, constrained by its original design and the processing capabilities of the time, could not accommodate the increased dimensionality resulting from distinguishing males and females. One of the objectives of the current model development and enhancement effort is to combine males and females into a single model.

constraints can be imposed on the monthly availability of a given characteristic group's accessions. For example, a composition constraint used during a recent analysis requires that 67 percent of each year's accessions come from male high school graduates in mental category I-IIIA. A seasonal constraint might require a percentage of those accessions to come in July.

The objective of the inventory projection is to determine the number of accessions needed to minimize monthly operating strength deviation while conforming to all composition and seasonal constraints. No month carries more weight than any other month, and the optimal number of accessions over the 84-month period may lead to positive or negative deviations in specific months. Constraints can be imposed to ensure that these deviations remain within acceptable bounds.

Model results are used in three general areas. The main hard-copy output of ELIM, the AAMMP, is used by various personnel management organizations to find the current and future status of enlisted inventory. In this role, the AAMMP is a primary document in the determination of the POM and the budget. ELIM output also provides the monthly accession goals, both by quantity and type of recruit, to the Recruiting Command. Finally, ELIM outputs are input to MOSLS, where they act as aggregate constraints on MOSLS training pipeline projections.

An overview of the ELIM architecture is shown in Figure A.2. The modeling process involves the following four steps:

1. Prepare model inputs,
2. Project enlisted inventory,
3. Determine optimal accession levels, and
4. Produce model output.

Before describing each of these steps, we discuss the level of data detail encompassed within ELIM.

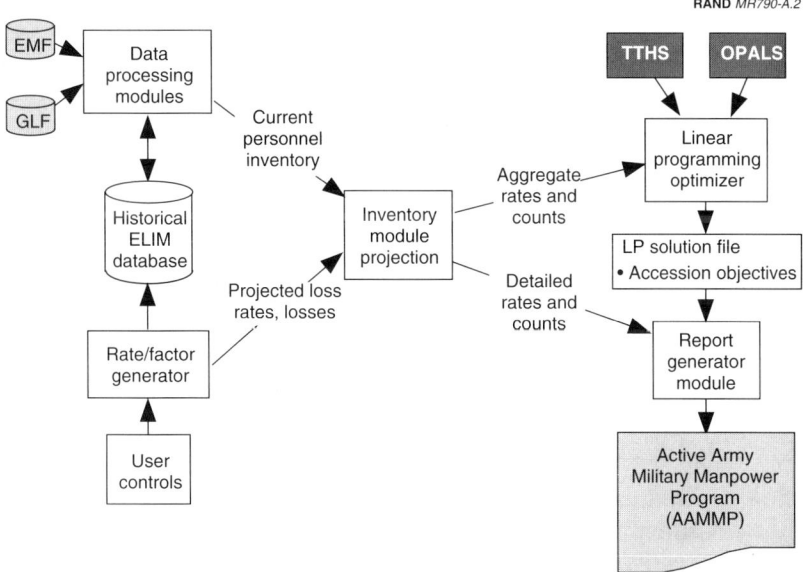

Figure A.2—Overview of ELIM Architecture

DATA DETAIL

Although ELIM manages the enlisted force at the aggregate level, it produces interim results and tracks personnel at a fairly disaggregate level. It does this by defining a number of Characteristic Groups (C-groups) for personnel in their first enlistment term and by differentiating "careerists" (those personnel who have reenlisted or extended beyond their first term) by the year of service (YOS) and the number of months until the end of the current enlistment contract (ETS). ELIM tracks the number of personnel in these various groupings as it projects the force into the future.

C-groups are defined along several dimensions, including gender (male or female), education level (high school graduate [HSDG] or non-high school graduate [NHSDG]), and Armed Forces Qualification Test (AFQT) test score category (categories I to V, distinguishing between IIIA and IIIB). Within these categories, the term of the enlisted contract (two to six years) and the expected training time are also tracked. The definition of the various C-groups is shown in Table A.1.

The C-groups for first-term personnel and the months to ETS and year-of-service tracking for the careerists are important categorizations in the model for two reasons. First, ELIM addresses gains and losses over time. Analysis of historical loss rates suggests that retention behavior varies for different types, or groups, of people. For example, personnel who score in the higher AFQT categories typically stay in the force longer than those who score in the lower categories. Also, the retention rate tends to increase, up to a point, as the years of service increase.

The second reason for the various data groupings is that the Army is particularly interested in certain groups of enlisted personnel and thus manages them more intensively. Females are an example. High school graduates and high test score personnel are tracked because of the relationship between a person's education and his or her ability to be effectively trained.

In addition to calculating loss rates for the separate categories, constraints within the optimization model reflect the C-groups. These constraints are used to bound the number of accessions within certain groups. For example, constraints may specify the maximum

Table A.1

Characteristic Groups Used for First-Term Personnel

C-Group	Gender	Education	Test Score Category	Term (Years)	Training Time (months)
1	Male	HSDG	I–IIIA	3,4	2–13
2	Male	HSDG	IIIB	3,4	2–13
3	Male	HSDG	IV–V	3,4	2–13
4	Male	NHSDG	I–IIIA	3,4	2–13
5	Male	NHSDG	IIIB–V	3,4	2–13
6	Female	HSDG	I–IIIA	3,4	2–13
7	Female	HSDG	IIIB–V	3,4	2–13
8	Female	NHSDG	All	3,4	2–13
9	Male	All	All	2,5,6	
10	Female	All	All	2,5,6	

NOTE: Both Variable Enlistment Length (VEL) program and non-VEL enlistees are included in C-groups 1 through 8.

percentage of non-high school graduates that the Army is willing to recruit, or the minimum number of females in the force.

The disaggregate nature of the data from the various groupings results in additional model detail. This additional detail increases the complexity of the model and adds to the model's execution time. The current effort to develop a new version of ELIM is reexamining the various groupings of personnel that should be tracked and managed more intensively.

PREPARATION OF MODEL INPUT

ELIM maintains a database containing 48 months of personnel strength and transaction data for career soldiers and 72 months for first-term enlisted personnel. This database is used to calculate the various rates for ELIM. The Gain and Loss File (GLF) has records for all the personnel transactions (accessions, losses by type of loss, and reenlistments or extensions) during the previous month. These data become numerators in calculating loss rates and for determining distribution factors.[3] For the monthly ELIM runs, the GLF updates the historical database. The current month's transactions are supplied to the database, replacing the oldest set of data.

The Enlisted Master File (EMF) is the other major file that provides data to ELIM. The EMF has a record for every enlisted person in the Army, and thus provides a snapshot of the current personnel strength. This snapshot shows the number of personnel in the various data groupings along with their expiration of term of service dates. Therefore, the EMF also provides the denominators for loss rate calculations.

The GLF, EMF, and historical databases provide the starting point for ELIM to (1) project the current personnel inventory into the future and (2) calculate the various loss rates needed for that projection. Since these data are the starting point and the means for inventory projection, it is important that the data in the EMF and the GLF be accurate and up-to-date. Inaccurate or missing data affect the re-

---

[3]There are distribution factors for nonprior service accessions by term and training times within C-group, prior service accessions by month of service and term, and extensions by length of contract.

ported number of personnel in the force and, therefore, the number of new recruits necessary to balance force manning. Errors in this part of the process affect end strength calculations and, therefore, the budget. Because of the magnitude of the personnel budget, small variations between forecasts and actual can result in several hundreds of millions of dollars difference between budget estimates and the actual dollars needed in personnel accounts.

RATE CALCULATIONS

The ELIM database is used to calculate various rates and factors for the first-term and career data groups. These rates are used to predict various future transactions for the different groups, including losses by type of loss,[4] both prior-service (PS) and non–prior-service (NPS) gains, extensions, and reenlistments.

ELIM offers a range of statistical techniques for calculating the rates. These techniques include exponential smoothing, weighted averages, exponential least-squares fitting, and exponential target phasing. Although all these methods are available, exponential smoothing is typically used to produce rates from the historical data.

Exponential smoothing uses the following general equation:

$$f(t+1) = f(t) + \alpha * [r(t) - f(t)]$$

where $f(t+1)$ = the forecast rate for the next time period,
  $f(t)$ = the forecast rate for the current time period that was made in the previous time period,
  $r(t)$ = the actual rate for the current time period,
  α = a smoothing constant between 0 and 1.

The relationship bases the future rate on a linear combination of the current rate and the magnitude of the error in predicting the current rate. That is, if the current rate exactly equals the value predicted in the previous time period, the predicted rate for the next time period

---

[4]Losses are defined for the following categories: dropped from strength, entry-level separation, unsatisfactory performance, other adverse causes, physical disability, marriage, pregnancy, parenthood, and dependency, early retirement, ETS losses, and other losses.

would be the actual rate for the current time period. On the other hand, if the current rate is greater (or lesser) than the rate that was predicted in the previous time period, the current forecast for the next time period is increased (or decreased) by an amount specified by the smoothing constant and the margin of error. The smoothing constant, α, is set close to one if more importance (weight) is placed on the error and closer to zero if less importance (weight) is placed on the error.

The future rates are typically based solely on historical transactions. ELIM does not contain mechanisms to incorporate behavioral factors or the effects of variables external to the Army. For example, a shift in the ratio of military-to-civilian pay or in the civilian employment rates has been shown to influence the propensity of people to join or stay in the military. Nor does ELIM have feedback loops. Changes in Army policies such as the promotion rates may have a positive or negative influence on reenlistment rates, but ELIM does not model these effects. These types of behavioral relationships are typically the subject of the econometric models used in other personnel functional areas, such as recruiting and retention.

ELIM does allow user controls that can reflect behavioral factors. An ELIM user can specify that rates in a certain time period or for a length of time be adjusted upward or downward. Such adjustments may be warranted based on current or future changes in external variables or because the Army has adjusted policies and practices in an attempt to influence (either positively or negatively) recruiting and retention rates. For example, an Army decision to change reenlistment bonuses can be reflected through the user controls by increasing or decreasing the historical retention rate. The user can also identify previous time periods in which the transactions should be eliminated or adjusted when calculating future rates. This control was used to adjust the personnel transactions during the Gulf War because of the various "stop loss" policies implemented at the time.

The current inventory levels based on the EMF and the various rates and factors are provided to the ELIM Inventory Projection Module (IPM) to predict future personnel strengths.

USING SIMULATION TO PROJECT PERSONNEL INVENTORY

ELIM uses a deterministic, fixed time step simulation to predict future personnel inventory levels given the current force, historical transition rates of various personnel groups into and out of the inventory, and the future outcomes of previous actions and policies. The simulation has no stochastic or probabilistic properties; the same set of inputs produces the same output. The simulation advances time in one-month increments, at each step calculating expected gains and losses across the various data groupings.

For the short term, the simulation projects the expected outcomes of events that have occurred in previous time periods. For example, from data in the EMF, the simulation determines how many soldiers reach their ETS point in each future month (and the expected number who will reenlist or extend at that point and for every month prior to that point). Also, the simulation has access to the future output of training pipelines. Therefore, the short-term inventory predictions are largely "fixed" by past decisions and are difficult for the Army to adjust by changing policies or increasing resource levels.

In addition to projecting losses from the starting inventory for the short term, the simulation also estimates future (long-term) accessions based on historical rates and projects proportional losses from those anticipated future accessions.

The steps in the force projection, or aging, cycle appear in Figure A.3. Starting with the current inventory in each C-group for first-termers and by year of service for careerists, the simulation first calculates expected new prior service and nonprior service accessions. These accessions, estimated based on historical average rates, are an initial prediction of new personnel who will come into the force. These initial estimates will be refined and the ultimate recruiting goals will be set by the optimization program.

For the current force and the new accessions, the number of reenlistments or extensions, attrition losses for any of several reasons, and normal separation for those soldiers at their ETS point are esti-

Description of ELIM 55

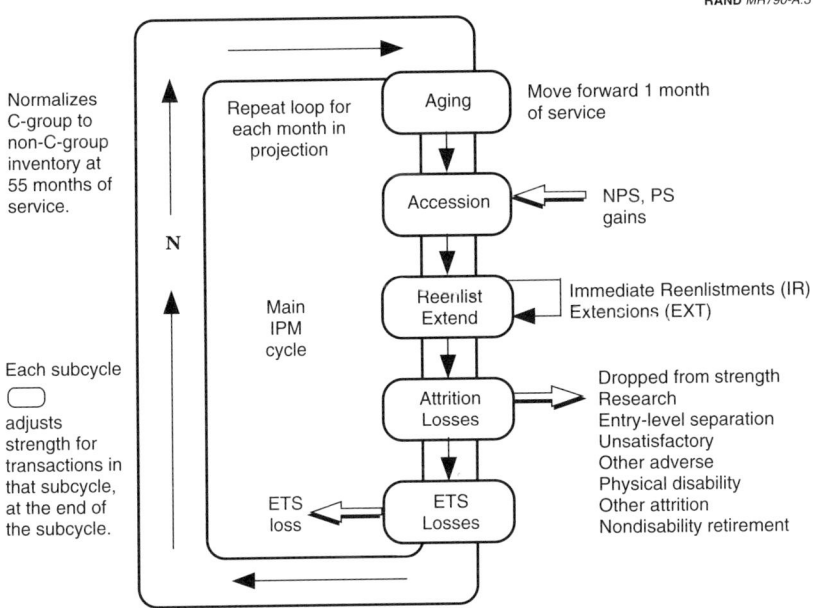

Figure A.3—Simulation Projects Inventory

mated based on the historical rates for each C-group and YOS.[5] The simulation then makes all the necessary additions, subtractions, and future adjustments and ages the force one month. The cycle continues for seven years into the future.

The simulation produces two sets of output files—one containing aggregate rates and counts that is provided to the optimization routine, and a second containing detailed C-group and YOS data that is provided to the output generator.

---

[5]As the C-groups progress through time, they are converted to the YOS career categories at 55 months of service. That is, retention rates are tracked by C-group for the first enlistment term because rates vary significantly during that period. Beyond the first reenlistment point, retention rates are tracked by year of service and ETS.

USING OPTIMIZATION TO BALANCE THE FORCE

In the next step of the ELIM process, a linear programming model determines the optimal set of enlisted accessions required to meet the operating strength objectives over the seven-year horizon. These accessions, simultaneously determined for each C-group and projection month, are constrained by recruiting objectives for each C-group and seasonal effects on the availability of potential enlistees in each C-group. The model also balances groups by tracking the flow of personnel through the system.[6]

Several sources provide input data for the optimization module. The TTHS model provides data on the number of personnel in overhead accounts, including soldiers in the training pipelines. The OPALS model provides officer data (e.g., estimated strengths, gains, losses, and overhead accounts). The optimization module uses the data from these two models to partition the total number of people in the inventory (i.e., the total strength) into those in operating units (i.e., operating strength) and those in the individuals account and to distinguish between the number of enlisted and the number of officers.

The simulation module provides the aggregate numbers of enlisted personnel and their aggregate transition rates into and out of the force. Finally, the user provides the force structure allowance (FSA), data on other sources of personnel, such as cadets at the United States Military Academy, values for the recruiting and entry-level training constraints, and other optional inputs that shape the objective function and constraints within the optimization module.[7]

Although there are several possible objective functions, the one used the majority of the time is to minimize the weighted sum of the over- and understrengths relative to the force structure allowance.[8] That

---

[6] The model also can use budget constraints for the total force and constraints on the entry-level training base. This capability is not currently used.

[7] There is typically a data call and subsequent meeting among the various personnel organizations that provide data to ELIM. This monthly process informs the various groups of the values that will be used or that are needed for the upcoming ELIM iteration. It helps ensure agreement on the correct values for different constraints and other factors in the model.

[8] Other objective functions available to the user include minimizing the (unweighted) total operating strength deviation over the seven-year period, the number of reserve

is, the optimization module is typically used to minimize the difference between "faces" and "spaces" where larger differences result in more severe "costs" or penalties. The nature of the penalties associated with excessive deviations from the FSA are shown in Figure A.4.[9]

The penalty weight for each month forces the calculated operating strength to be as close as possible to the FSA provided by the user. A smaller penalty is used for "acceptable" deviations (either over or under) and a higher one is used for "excessive" deviations. For both sets, the same weight is used for both positive and negative deviations (that is, there is not a separate weight for overstrength and a different weight for understrength).

The optimization module has three general types of constraints—force structure balancing, entry-level training capacities, and accession related. The force structure balancing constraints represent the flow of personnel among the various accounts and data groupings or the subtotaling of specific types of personnel (e.g., total nonprior service) across the various data groups. The accession-related constraints specify limits on the number of people who can be recruited each month (i.e., seasonal impacts on recruiting) and the minimum or maximum number of personnel in various C-groups (e.g., the minimum number of high school degree graduates, females, or high-quality personnel, measured by test score). These latter constraints shape the types of accessions desired while restricting the maximum number who can be recruited each month.

The optimization module produces the monthly accession objectives, by personnel type (i.e., C-group). These data are passed to the report generator to produce various output reports and to the MOSLS model, where they act as constraints on the monthly gains and losses in various MOSLS routines.

---

component personnel on active duty, the number of NPS accessions over all C-groups and months, deviations from the end of fiscal year targets, or the deviation from total man-year targets.

[9]Penalties, although available, are not used currently. All deviations from the target carry the same weight.

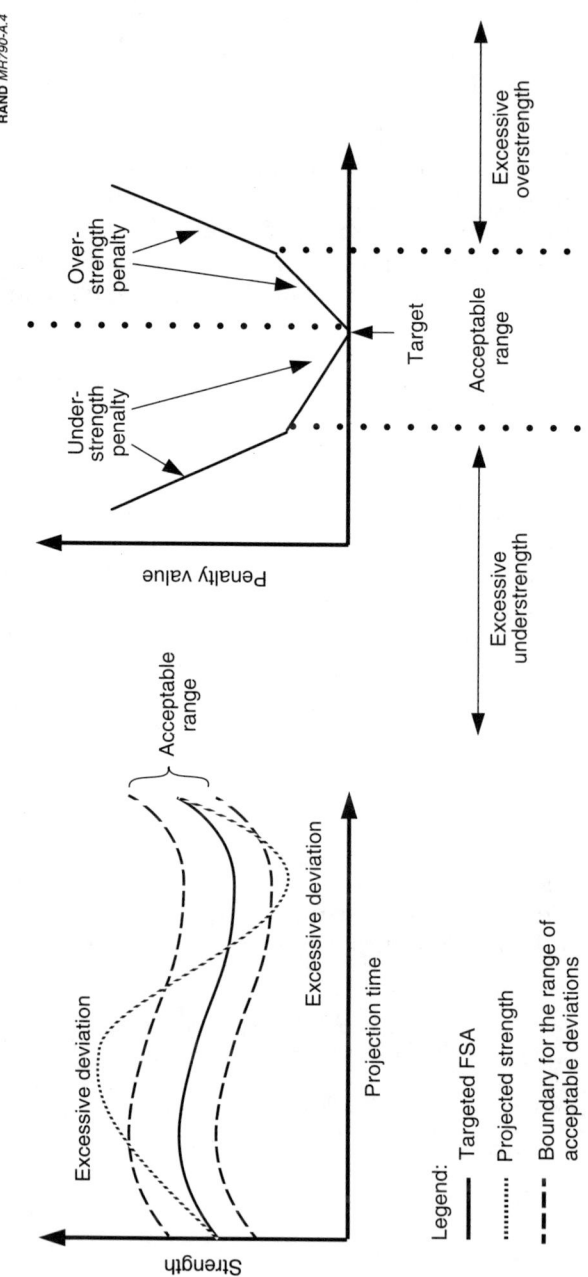

Figure A.4—Objective Function and Optimization Criteria

MODEL OUTPUT

The simulation and the optimization modules provide their output data to the ELIM report generator module. This module organizes and summarizes the data in various ways to produce a variety of output reports and displays. Primary among these is the AAMMP, the principal Army document to support the POM, the OSD, and President's Budget Submissions.[10] ELIM output also provides information on accession and reenlistment policies.

The AAMMP provides a seven-year projection by month and includes both enlisted and officer data. The AAMMP includes a summary of the assumptions and constraints used for the ELIM run and charts comparing the present projections with those of several previous monthly ELIM runs. It provides a wide range of data on trained and operating strengths, man-years, the individuals account, gains, losses, and extensions. It provides these data for the various C-groups, YOS groups, and female soldiers.

ELIM (and TTHS) also produces interface files of aggregate strength, gain, and loss data for the MOSLS model and the ATRRS, as well as data for a menu-driven Management Information System (MIS) that is used for *ad hoc* queries. Finally, the ELIM report generator produces a number of other historical data summaries, graphs, and charts.

An important part of the output process is a monthly meeting of representatives from the various personnel organizations at which the key results of ELIM are discussed and reviewed. This so-called "Gong Brief" is an arena in which the personnel community can interact to shape personnel goals and policies. It allows the various organizations to identify potential problems and to suggest changes to the ELIM recommendations (which may result in a new run of the model).

---

[10]TTHS and FELIM also provide data for the AAMMP.

SUMMARY

ELIM is a useful, and key, tool for Army active enlisted strength management. Its main advantage lies in its integration of several personnel functional activities. By relating recruiting, training, and retention at the aggregate level, it provides an organized process for addressing strength management issues.

ELIM uses valid analytical techniques in a proper way given the original and current uses of the model. Its short-term predictions are typically accurate. The long-term predictions are also accurate during periods of little change in the Army's structure and policies and in the external variables that affect personal behaviors (e.g., civilian wage and employment rates). The monthly updates help to adjust the model's predictions and refine prior forecasts.

It is important to remember that ELIM's optimization module reflects the policies necessary to achieve the specified future force structure manpower goals. Predictions of future values are based on the assumption that the accession levels and various transition rates are actually attained. If the policies incorporated in the model are not followed, the model's future predictions will vary from actual events.

ELIM does, however, have a number of limitations. Because the model was built over two decades ago and has been substantially modified over time, it is fairly opaque, making it difficult to comprehend its structure and flow. In this regard, ELIM is not "user-friendly," although the Army's multiyear effort to develop a replacement for ELIM should correct this limitation.

ELIM is fairly complex because of the numerous data groupings and rates that are used to transition the groups into, through, and out of the personnel system. It was built and is used primarily for programming purposes. It can be used for planning studies, but its complexity and lack of transparency can hinder an inexperienced analyst's ability to do "what-if" types of analyses. Although providing quicker turnaround than other models, such as MOSLS, it still takes two hours or longer for an ELIM run. Again, run times should be shortened with the use of more modern software and algorithmic procedures.

Strength management addresses large magnitude policies and programs. The active end strength includes approximately half a million soldiers with a military personnel budget of approximately $20 billion. Although ELIM is fairly accurate in its predictions, especially in the short term, a small percentage over or under estimate can result in a several hundred million dollar difference between the estimated and actual military personnel budget.

Finally, ELIM is but one part of an overall process. It can help policymakers determine how best to achieve future goals, but the whole process depends on when and how policies are changed or implemented in addition to how the propensities of people to enter or stay in the Army change.

Appendix B
DESCRIPTION OF MOSLS

This appendix describes the model the Army uses to provide the details of military occupational specialty (MOS) and grade to Army enlisted personnel management.

BACKGROUND

Military Occupational Specialty Level System (MOSLS) is the model used by ODCSPER and PERSCOM to balance the MOS and grade-level requirements of the Army with the available population. It complements ELIM in that it provides grade and MOS detail, which ELIM does not consider.

MOSLS supports enlisted personnel policy at two levels. At the most aggregate level, MOSLS enables Army analysts to explore the implications of policies and behaviors that affect the Service's need for total numbers of individuals of certain skills and grades. MOSLS also supports the analysis of voluntary loss behavior and of involuntary loss policies upon the entire enlisted force. At the more detailed MOS and grade level, MOSLS results can be used to assess the effects of promotion, reenlistment, and accession policies. In addition MOSLS forecasts the Service's need for newly trained individuals by skill and helps determine the training programs necessary to produce such individuals.

MOSLS is one system within the Army strength management family of models, resources, and products. Figure B.1 shows how MOSLS interacts with ELIM, other models, and data systems.

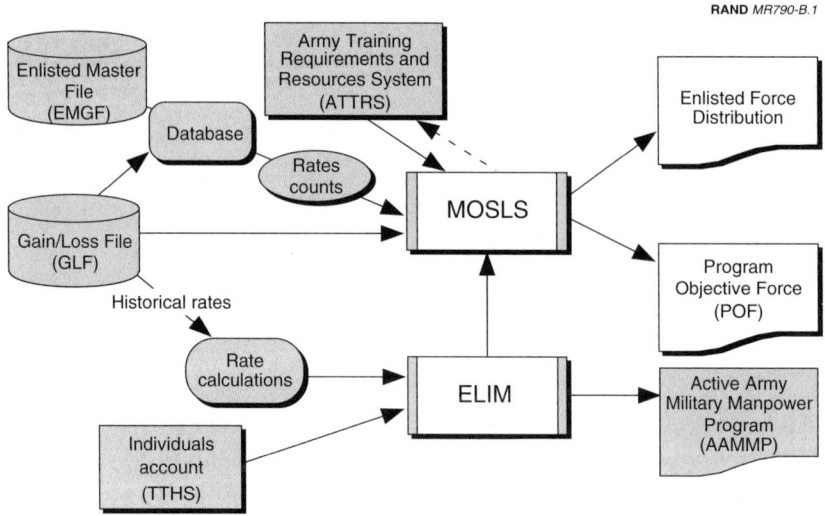

Figure B.1—Relation of MOSLS to Other Models and Databases

GENERAL ANALYTIC APPROACH AND ARCHITECTURE

Like ELIM, MOSLS uses both optimization and simulation to consider the ways the personnel community can control the enlisted force, the constraints upon various management options, and events beyond the control of the Service. The optimization function prescribes the best set of personnel management actions for what the Army can control, such as promotion, reclassification, and forced losses. The optimization models consider legal, resource, and budget constraints when determining the best sets of policies.

Simulation models are used to predict the behavior of the force beyond the Army's control. Simulation provides a more accurate representation of the future force by replicating probable loss, aging patterns, and training graduation rates, which management policies cannot directly alter.

This appendix discusses the three primary elements of MOSLS: the pre-processor module and its inputs, the trained strength model, and the post-processor module. Figure B.2 provides a schematic of the architecture and how its components relate to each other. In general, the pre-processor determines the targets to which the model should optimize and the constraints that limit the optimization. It also includes the training simulation model, which projects how many individuals will be graduating from each skill training course. The trained strength model is a large network model that uses the trained output of the training simulation model and the targets and constraints of the pre-processor to model the most optimal force achievable. The post-processor includes the training requirements model, which considers the optimal force output from the trained strength model and reconsiders how the training simulation model should have allocated individuals across the skill training course. The post-processor also compiles the various output reports from MOSLS. The key outputs of MOSLS are the Enlisted Force Distribution and the Program Objective Force.

As Figure B.2 indicates, MOSLS contains three models: the training simulation model, the trained strength model, and the training requirements model. The interaction of the three models is central to the optimization process. The training simulation model begins the process by making a first estimate of the output from the MOS training pipelines over the 84 months of inventory projection. It considers what is current in each pipeline (and therefore cannot be changed) and estimates future pipeline production. This estimate is a "first guess" because the training simulation model does not have an accurate picture of promotions and losses over the 84-month projection.

The second model, the trained strength model, completes that picture. It takes the forecasts of the training simulation model and combines them with promotions, reclassifications, and losses to produce a detailed (grade, MOS, YOS) inventory projection. The model attempts to minimize the differences between the MOS requirements and inventory, adjusting promotions and reclassifications to do so.

When the projection is completed, the trained strength model looks at the MOS differences. If some difference are too large, the model adjusts training pipeline production, promotion, reclassification and forced loss rates, repeats the projection, reexamines MOS differ-

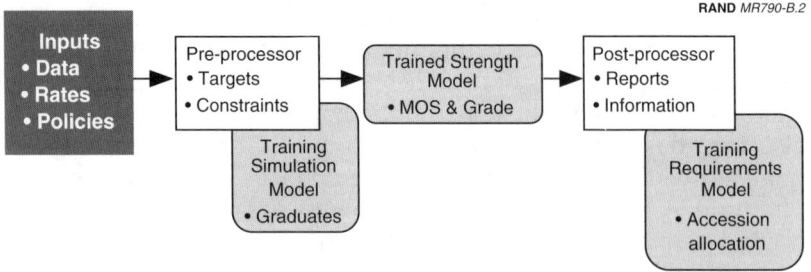

Figure B.2—MOSLS Architecture

ences, makes adjustments, and repeats the projection. This iterative process continues until MOS differences do not improve iteration to iteration.

The third model, the training requirements model, takes the results of the trained strength model (specifically, the adjusted MOS training pipeline production) and determines what input is necessary to the MOS training pipelines to meet the detailed force structure requirements. The training simulation model and the training requirements model differ in the following way. On the one hand, the training simulation model takes annual accessions and makes an initial attempt at allocating those accessions to the various MOS training pipelines. The training requirements model, on the other hand, works backward. Given the results of the trained strength model, it determines what the accession allocation to the MOS training pipelines must be to meet the force structure requirements, effectively adjusting the initial attempt at allocation of the training simulation model.

The Pre-Processor

Inputs. The pre-processor accepts inputs in the form of data, rates, and policies; it provides targets and constraints for the next element of MOSLS. MOSLS accepts data input from several sources. The Enlisted Master File extract provides detailed information about the current enlisted force. The Gain/Loss File extract is an account of the actual gains and losses from the enlisted service updated on a monthly basis. These two files provide input for MOSLS. They also are both used to compute loss and accession rates for the ELIM model. The output from the ELIM model is used to normalize the MOSLS total losses by category. The categories are ETS, retirement, and other.

Force structure and authorization data inputs, available in the PAM, provide the total number of units and the type and number of personnel authorizations by grade and MOS. Total strength and accessions data output from ELIM are also input to the MOSLS pre-processor. In addition, the Army Training Requirements and Resources System (ATRRS) provides detailed data about training schedule, the length of each class, the probable attrition or graduate rates, and the personnel currently in the skill training pipeline.

Policies that are user input to the pre-processor include relative priorities placed upon certain MOS, information about changing requirements for MOS, and forced loss or other programs that would affect the retention behavior of the force. Other personnel policies, such as planned reclassifications and forced loss programs are also inputs.

The policies input to the pre-processor are used in conjunction with the data inputs to determine the target, or optimal, force by grade and MOS that the model should strive to create. Thus, the target force, or trained strength targets, reflect policies such as priorities on certain MOS as well as authorizations for spaces, the numbers and types of soldiers in the individuals account,[1] and soldiers in space imbalanced MOS.[2]

---

[1] The individuals account generally includes TTHS, or trainees, transients, holdees, and students. It represents everyone who is not assigned to a unit, including prisoners and hospitalized individuals. Because MOSLS does include skill training, however, it accounts for individuals in the training pipeline, and these calculations to add the individuals account add only the additional THS. The size of the future individuals account is given in the ELIM interface file. MOSLS receives counts of the aggregate THS, which are broken down by grade counts using three years of historical data. The by-grade THS counts are used to modify the data to create the API (Authorizations Plus Individuals) targets used by the model.

[2] When MOS are designated solely for overseas duty, such as 4GR (Radio Broadcast Journalist), CONUS billets are designed to provide a rotation billet. These space-imbalanced MOS billets are added to the MOSLS target force in the pre-processor.

These inputs are manipulated to constrain the future system. Such constraints include short-term promotion bounds; any legislative restrictions, such as the legal limits on the number of E9s allowed; and budget constraints.

MOSLS has over 300,000 rates, based mostly upon MOS, grade, and YOS, which are input to the model. These rates will constrain the movement across the large network model in MOSLS that optimizes the future force. This will be discussed in more detail later. Table B.1 provides an example of many types of MOSLS rates and the basis by which they are applied. For example, the loss rates used for the trained strength force between grades E3 and E6 are applied to individuals by MOS, grade, YOS (within six months), years to ETS (within six months), and type of loss (e.g., mandated separations, directed separations, voluntary separations, death, etc.). These rates are managed by a database subsystem.

MOSLS rates are calculated based on a weighted average of the past 36 months.[3] The more recent data is weighted more heavily. ELIM uses a different process, which employs exponential smoothing of up to 48 months of detail. Thus, the ELIM and the MOSLS rates are different, but a normalization process brings the final result of the calculations within MOSLS in line with those calculated by ELIM using

Table B.1

MOSLS Rates and Factors

Rates	Factors
Trained strength loss (E3–E6)	MOS, Grade, 1/2 YOS, 1/2 YETS, Type
Trained strength loss (E7–E9)	MOS, Grade, YOS, Type
Trainee loss	MOS, Type
Promotion (E3–E5)	MOS, Grade, 1/2 YOS
Promotion (E6–E8)	Grade, TIG, YOS
Reclassification	MOS, Grade, Type
THS factors	MOS, Grade
Immediate Reenlistment factors	MOS, Grade
NPS TOS factors	MOS

---

[3]Weighted averages are calculated by applying a factor to each of the numbers averaged. The factors sum to 1.0. The larger the factor relative to the other factors, the more influence that number will have upon the calculated average.

different rates. Most of the 300,000 rates used by MOSLS cannot be altered by the user.

Functions of Pre-processor. The pre-processor uses the inputs provided to determine grade limits, estimate MOS trained strength targets, provide inputs for projections, and match monthly accessions to the training schedule.

The "spaces" authorizations do not include every individual in the Service. Thus, MOSLS calculates grade limits to include personnel not assigned to units by considering the individuals account of transients, prisoners, and hospitalized personnel in addition to the authorized "spaces." The calculated grade limits also reflect legal constraints, such as the limits on the number of E9s in the force, and budgetary constraints.

The MOS trained strength targets are calculated in the pre-processor as an input to the rest of MOSLS. These MOS targets comprise the optimal force for planning purposes. The targets are based upon the sum of authorized spaces to fill, the planned future individuals account,[4] and the space-imbalanced MOS (SIMOS). These SIMOS are positions created to provide a CONUS rotation for a given specialty, such as air defense, which would otherwise exist primarily overseas.

Training Simulation Model. The pre-processor also includes the training simulation model, which optimizes the incoming accessions across the existing training class programs. This embedded model considers the incoming accessions; personnel already in the training pipeline; the length of the training session; and the graduation, recycle, and retrain rates in allocating accessions to training programs and projecting the number of graduates. For example, in Figure B.3, the ATRRS might provide information about the training schedule, which informs MOSLS that for MOS A through E there are 300, 300, 300, 400, 50 training seats available, respectively. The training simulation model allocates the incoming 1000 accessions (as per ELIM's accessions numbers) across those seats.[5] The result might be that shown in the figure, which results in 200 accessions attending the

---

[4]Based upon a weighted average of the historical by-grade distribution of the THS account.
[5]Priority is given to small classes, to ensure that they are filled.

training of each of the first three MOSs, 350 accessions attending the training for MOS D, and 50 accessions in MOS E training. Then the training simulation model applies the information provided by ATRRS on the probable attrition and graduation rates of these accessions to determine the probable number of trained graduates for each of these MOSs. Thus, the final column in Figure B.3 indicates that a total of 800 newly trained individuals will result from this allocation across MOS training courses.

The model does not currently recognize monthly training limitations. In other words, although there are 300 training seats available for MOS A on an annual basis, this quota may result from three scheduled classes of 100 seats each. The current version of the training simulation model in MOSLS might assign 200 of the annual quota in the first month. Soon, however, MOSLS will interface with the PAM seats-available file and will be bound by monthly minimum and maximum training assignments.

Trained Strength Model

The trained strength model is the main element of MOSLS. This portion of the model strives to create the target force defined by the

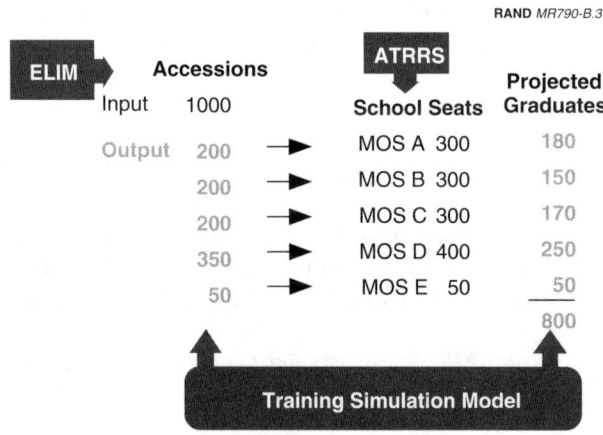

Figure B.3—Operation of Training Simulation Model

pre-processor, given the constraints interpreted in the pre-processor and the data inputs manipulated there. The trained strength model takes the trained individuals projected by the training simulation model and provides forecasts by fiscal year of the levels of MOS trained strength, losses, and newly trained individuals. It also prescribes promotions, reclassifications, MOS conversions, and other policies that will produce the optimal force.

The trained strength model produces this output from the calculations of a large-scale network model, which optimizes across policy decisions such as promotion and then simulates individual behaviors to forecast the resulting force out to seven years. The resulting force is compared with the targeted force, and the optimization process is repeated to reduce the difference between the two. Then the model once again simulates the passage of time to produce seven years of forecasts. The optimization routine is repeatedly conducted to minimize the deviation between the target levels and the forecast numbers across MOS and grades. In other words, the model will prescribe transactions, such as promotion, simulate individual behaviors, such as reenlistment, and then compare the resulting answer to a defined optimal target. The next iteration of prescribed transactions and simulated behaviors will produce an answer closer to the target. These cycles are repeated approximately 10 times until the difference between successive model runs is minimal.

Because the network model considers approximately 30 different management transactions (e.g., promotion, reclassification, conversion) across 1,500 different MOSs and grades, for a total of seven years, this portion of MOSLS takes considerable time to run. The run time required for the trained strength model is 22 to 24 hours.

The operation of the trained strength model employs a series of "nodes and arcs." The nodes represent groups of individuals and the arcs represent transactions, or movement between these groups. Figure B.4 depicts these relationships.

For example, an arc connecting a node labeled "MOS A g1" to "MOS A g2" represents the promotion of an individual from grade 1 to grade 2 while retaining the same MOS. Likewise, movement from "MOS A g1" to "MOS B g1" would occur if an individual changed his skill designator from MOS A to MOS B without being promoted

72 Relating Resources to Personnel Readiness

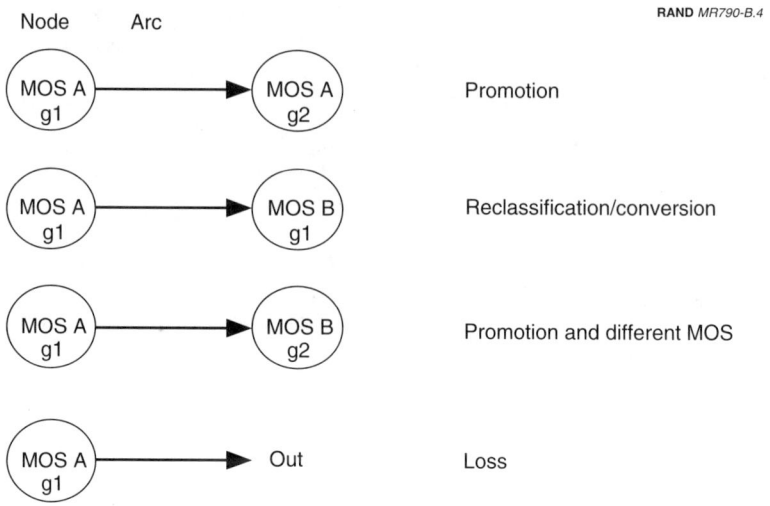

Figure B.4—Relationships between Nodes and Arcs

(remaining grade 1). Movement that denotes both promotion and a change of skill designator could be represented with movement from "MOS A g1" to "MOS B g2." These are all examples of movements from nodes, which have targeted levels, across arcs, to different nodes, which also have targeted levels. Another kind of movement is that from any node out of the system. In this case, the destination is not another node. Instead, the individual is removed from the system to represent a separation.

These arcs have capacities that limit the movement from one node to another. Nodes connect with multiple arcs. Each arc has both a capacity level and an incentive associated with that capacity. The capacities are calculated relative to the destination node. For example, Figure B.5 shows the arcs to a node representing a high-priority MOS on the left, and those to a low-priority MOS node on the right. The capacity of the first arc to the high-priority MOS node is constrained to 98 percent of the target fill. Once that arc has transferred its limit, the model credits a 100-point incentive. The next 2 percent of the node target is carried by the next arc, which receives a credit of only 10 points. Thus, filling this node to its capacity results in a 110-point

Description of MOSLS 73

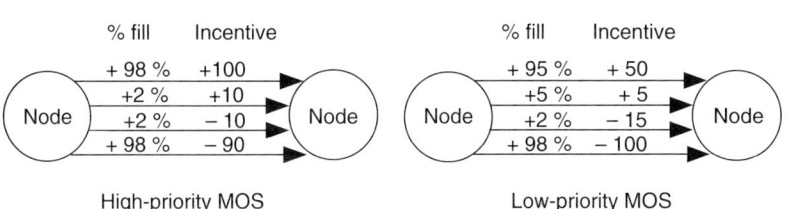

Figure B.5—How the Model Uses Incentives

incentive. In contrast, the first arc to the low-priority node is limited to only 95 percent of the target fill, and the model credits only a 50-point incentive. The second arc, which fills the low-priority node to its full capacity by providing the next 5 percent of its fill, receives only a 5-point incentive.

During a model run, the model will fill the first arc of the high-incentive node to receive the most incentive points. The model will then strive to fill the first arc of the low-priority MOS, because the 50 incentive points of the first arc are worth more than the 10 incentive points that would be received by filling the high-priority node to full capacity.

The example arcs and nodes shown also indicate the value of filling all nodes to capacity before overfilling any. The third and fourth arcs in both of the examples carry excess individuals to the destination nodes. In both cases, the model takes away incentive points from the total when nodes are overfilled. Once again, if the model is compelled to overfill either of the nodes, it will overfill the high-priority node, because of the difference in negative incentive points. Should there be additional overflow, the model will determine if it is better to slightly overfill the low-priority node, and suffer a –15 incentive price, than further overfill the high-priority node at the cost of another –90 incentive points.

Each node in the trained strength model has targeted values, and each arc has an assigned capacity and an incentive value to meet that capacity. The users control the capacities and incentives of different nodes by placing relative fill priorities upon the nodes. In general, the noncommissioned officer (NCO) positions and the current year and nearer outyears have higher priorities than the lower ranking grades and later years.

The trained strength model is a large network of these node-to-node representations of personnel management transactions. Within each time period, individuals travel among the nodes. Figure B.6 represents some of the transactions within a time period. At the left, "MOS X g" represents the individuals of MOS X within grade g. Some of these individuals will continue in the same MOS and grade, and so are shown to the right, in a node of the same label. Others are reclassified, and move along arcs to the pool of people who are reclassified—mandatorily, voluntarily, with reenlistment, or because of model feasibility adjustments. Of that pool, some move into MOS X grade g.

Some individuals are reclassified with conversions and travel one of the arcs shown to MOS Z grade g. They might be Same-Grade Chart Reclassificatios (SGCR), which represent normal lateral career progressions. Some SGCR require training; these individuals travel a different arc. The other conversion arcs, one with training and one without, model the transfer of personnel inventory as directed by the manpower managers, such as an administrative change in MOS symbols or an addition or deletion of a MOS, and also force additional flows of individuals for other than normal lateral career progressions, such as to new equipment training.

Two additional inputs to the system are shown at the bottom of the figure. These represent individuals entering the system from the training pipeline and those entering with prior service who do not require training.

In the middle of the figure, some individuals of MOS X, grade g, are promoted. They either move to node MOS X of a higher grade than their previous mode, or they move into the promotion pool, from which they might change both their grade and their skill designator.

At the end of the time period, once all the individual movements across arcs are complete, the model advances a time period. At this time, the model calculates the incentives and disincentives recorded for the priority fills of each node. The model continues to advance in time periods and calculate incentive points. After each complete ad-

Description of MOSLS 75

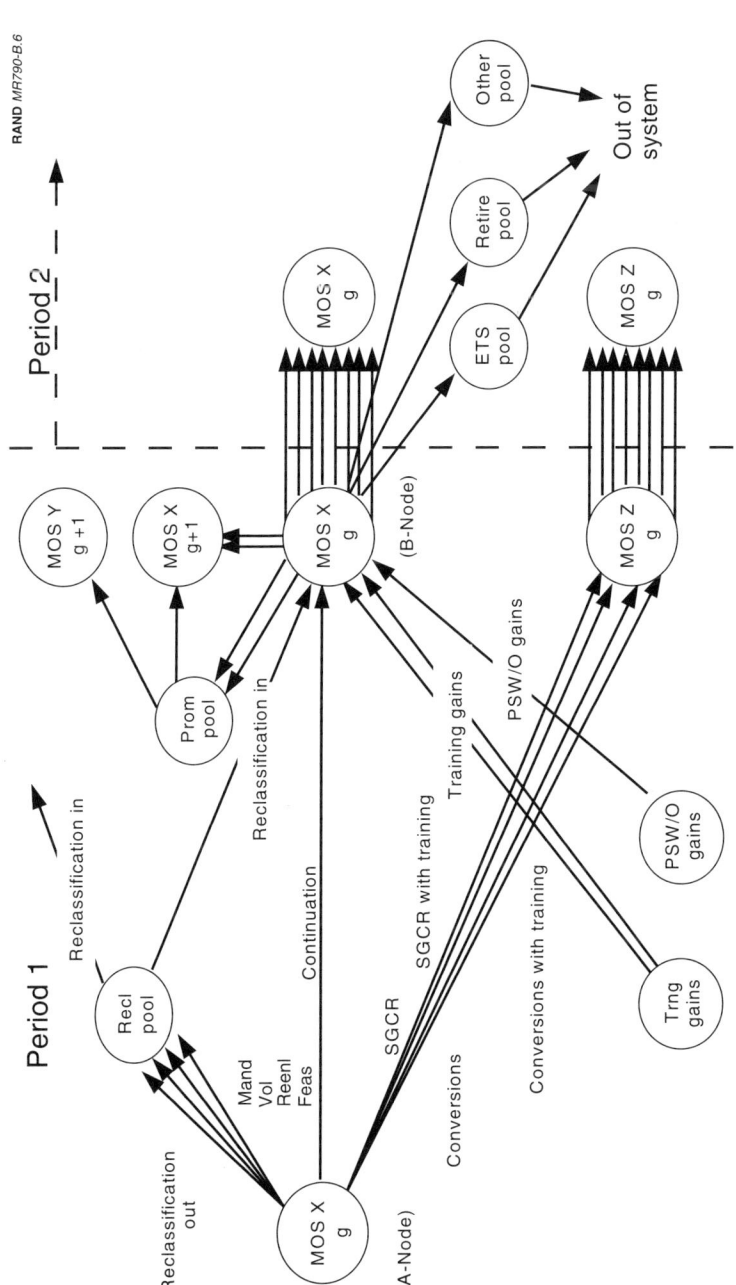

Figure B.6—Node and Arc Network of Trained Strength Model

vancement of seven years, the model returns to the current time period and modifies management actions to reduce the difference between the targeted force and the result of the last model run by maximizing the incentive points received in each run.

One of the personnel management transactions represented in MOSLS is promotion. Because promotions fall within the Army's control, they are optimized, not simulated; they do not occur automatically with the passage of simulated time. The promotions are constrained by several limiting factors. First, MOSLS recognizes from the current promotion lists that some individuals have already been identified for promotions in the near term. Second, promotion eligibility requirements limit who can be promoted to which grade. Finally, there are established grade limitations, such as the legislation that limits the percentage of the total enlisted force who can be E9s. However, the budgetary constraints are more stringent than the legislative limits, so the model would promote individuals more generously than the current fiscal situation dictates were the model not also user-controlled to restrict promotions.

The MOSLS trained strength model optimizes across all the possible personnel management transactions, and then simulates the advance of time. The difference between the answer and the targeted optimal solution is considered by the model as it repeats the process with multiple iterations, until the difference between successive runs is marginal. The trained strength model currently takes 22 to 24 hours of run time to converge to the eventual answer.

The trained strength model can be placed in the context of the entire MOSLS process by returning to the summary that describes the output of the training simulation model. This process is represented in Figure B.7. The training simulation model distributes accessions across available MOS training programs and projects the number of graduates who will complete each program. The trained strength model takes those graduates as input to the trained force. Considering the MOS targets, the grade limits, the projected losses, and other management transactions, the trained strength model projects the eventual trained force. In so doing, it also notes the difference between this projected force and the desired optimal force. This difference is an input to the training requirements model, dis-

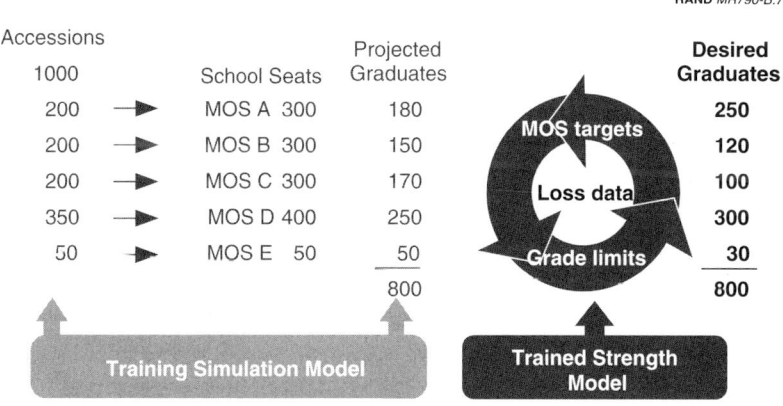

Figure B.7—Trained Strength Model

cussed below, which will reevaluate the original allocation of individuals across the training courses offered.

Post-Processor Module

The post-processor includes the training requirements model, which reexamines the optimal number of graduates that the trained strength model identified and reallocates the original accessions across the various skill training programs. This process is represented in Figure B.8. Although the training requirements model targets the total number of accessions originally identified by ELIM and input to MOSLS, it is not constrained to these numbers. Thus, the training requirements model recommends a total number of accessions, distributed across the training programs. The output from the training requirements model indicates where changes to the training program, either available seats within a skill or the schedule, are necessary. It will also indicate whether the ELIM accession figures are optimal.

The post-processor manipulates the output of the trained strength model to construct monthly breakouts, by MOS and grade, of such information as trained strength, losses, training graduates, promo-

78 Relating Resources to Personnel Readiness

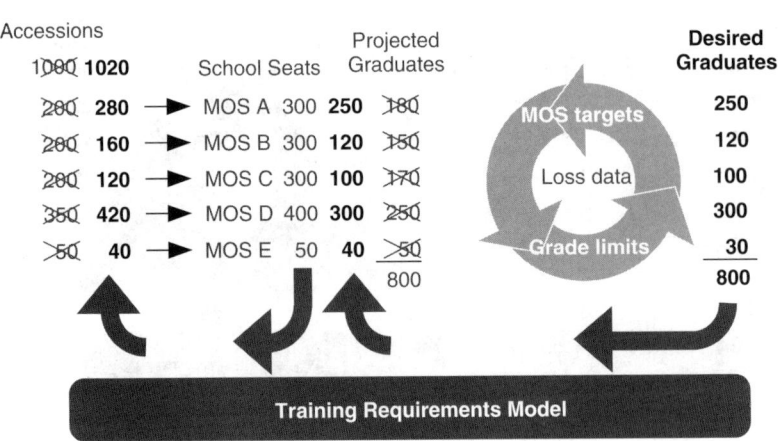

Figure B.8—Reallocation of Original Accessions

tions, reclassifications, and conversions. The post-processor also compiles totals by MOS, by career management field, by career management field with grades, by total Army, and by total Army with grades. It also manipulates the output to meet the requirements with the various MIS, interface files, and external systems with which MOSLS interfaces.

SUMMARY

Like ELIM, MOSLS is a useful tool for Army active enlisted strength management. The main advantage of MOSLS is its integration of multiple personnel functional activities, such as training, promotion, retention, and reclassification, with a tremendous degree of detail. MOSLS provides an organized process for trained strength management with detailed monthly updates to refine prior forecasts and observe the consequences of enlisted trained strength management policies.

Again like ELIM, the analytical techniques are valid and properly employed given the current use of the model. The short-term predictions are typically very accurate, and the long-term predictions are reasonably accurate given input assumptions about the changing environment and upcoming policy changes. The monthly runs and associated discussions help to accommodate changes in the Army environment or in other assumptions.

However, the optimization and simulation within MOSLS depend upon the quality of the input data and the assumptions that planned policy changes will be implemented and that unforeseen events or policy changes will not affect the enlisted force. If unexpected policy changes occur or if the policy decisions prescribed by prior MOSLS runs are not implemented, then the model runs will not accurately project the future enlisted force.

An additional limitation of MOSLS is the amount of run time and expertise required to conduct the monthly runs. Frequent "what-if" excursions are not a practical use of MOSLS, and it is unlikely that the Army will ever be able to conduct the monthly MOSLS runs independent of the civilian contractor. The MOSLS results are well documented and available in numerous data reports. However, the reports themselves are not always easily understandable, and the model processes that contributed to the results are opaque and require considerable expertise to explain. Again, the Army will probably not be able to sustain an internal expertise. The extraordinary number of calculations which so complicate MOSLS, however, also provide the level of detail that is so helpful to Army strength management. MOSLS is a valuable element in the strength management process.

REFERENCES

Andrews, Robert P., and James F. Shambo, *A System Dynamics Analysis of the Factors Affecting Combat Readiness*, Wright-Patterson Air Force Base, OH: Air Force Institute of Technology, LSSR 48-80, June 1980.

Antel, John, James R. Hosek, and Christine E. Peterson, *Military Enlistment and Attrition*, Santa Monica, CA: RAND, R-3510-FMP, June 1987.

Ardoin, Cy D., *Modeling and Simulation Information System (MSIS) User Manual*, Alexandria, VA: Institute for Defense Analyses, October 1993.

Armor, David J., R. L. Fernandez, K. Bers, D. S. Schwarzbach, S. C. Moore, and L. Cutler, *Recruit Aptitudes and Army Job Performance: Setting Enlistment Standards for Infantrymen*, Santa Monica, CA: RAND, R-2874-MRAL, September 1982.

Asch, Beth J., and James N. Dertouzos, *Educational Benefits Versus Enlistment Bonuses: A Comparison of Recruiting Options*, Santa Monica, CA: RAND, MR-302-OSD, 1994.

Asch, Beth J., and Bruce R. Orvis, *Recent Recruiting Trends and Their Implications: Preliminary Analysis and Recommendations*, Santa Monica, CA: RAND, MR-549-A/OSD, 1994.

Asch, Beth J., and John T. Warner, *A Policy Analysis of Alternative Military Retirement Systems*, Santa Monica, CA: RAND, MR-465-OSD, 1994.

Betts, Richard K., *Military Readiness: Concepts, Choices, Consequences*, Washington, DC: Brookings Institution, 1995.

Buddin, Richard, *The Role of Service Experience in Post-Training Attrition in the Army and Air Force*, Santa Monica, CA: RAND, R-2682-MRAL, November 1981.

Buddin, Richard, D. S. Levy, J. M. Hanley, and D. M. Waldman, *Promotion Tempo and Enlisted Retention*, Santa Monica, CA: RAND, R-4135-FMP, 1992.

Buddin, Richard, and Christina Witsberger, *Reducing the Air Force Male Enlistment Requirement: Effects on Recruiting Prospects of the Other Services*, Santa Monica, CA: RAND, R-3265-AF, March 1985.

Burnam, M. Audrey, L. S. Meredith, C. D. Sherbourne, R. B. Valdez, and G. Vernez, *Army Families and Soldier Readiness*, Santa Monica, CA: RAND, R-3884-A, 1992.

Campbell, Charlotte H., et al., *A Model of Family Factors and Individual and Unit Readiness: Literature Review*, Alexandria, VA: U.S. Army Research Institute for the Behavioral and Social Sciences, ARI Research Note 91-30, February 1991.

Clay-Mendez, Deborah, et al., *Balancing Accession and Retention*, Alexandria, VA: Center for Naval Analyses, CNS 1176, September 1982.

Collins, John M., *Military Preparedness: Principles Compared with U.S. Practices*, Washington, DC: Congressional Research Service, CRS Report for Congress 94-48 S, January 21, 1994.

Congressional Budget Office, *An Analysis of the President's Budgetary Proposals for Fiscal Year 1995*, Washington, DC, April 1994.

Congressional Budget Office, *Trends in Selected Indicators of Military Readiness, 1980 Through 1993*, Washington, DC, March 1994.

Cook, Alvin A., Jr., *Occupational Choice, the Draft, and the Excess Supply of Air Force Volunteers*, Santa Monica, CA: RAND, P-4606-1, November 1971.

Cook, Alvin A., Jr., *Quality Adjustment and the Excess Supply of Air Force Volunteers*, Santa Monica, CA: RAND, P-4711, September 1971.

Cook, A. A., Jr., and C. M. Rutherford, *A Computer Program and Model for Predicting the Supply of Air Force Volunteers*, Santa Monica, CA: RAND, R-910-PR, May 1972.

Cook, Alvin A., Jr., and John P. White, *Estimating the Quality of Airmen Recruits*, Santa Monica, CA: RAND, P-4763, January 1972.

Cotterman, Robert F., *Forecasting Enlistment Supply: A Time Series of Cross Sections Model*, Santa Monica, CA: RAND, R-3252-FMP, July 1986.

Curtin, Neal P., *Military Readiness: Current Indicators Need to Be Expanded for a More Comprehensive Assessment*, Washington, DC: United States General Accounting Office, T-NSIAD-94-160, April 21, 1994.

"Defense Department Special Briefing with Secretary of Defense William Perry and Joint Chiefs of Staff Chairman John Shalikashvili on Quality of Life Initiatives in the Military," Federal News Reuter Transcript Service, November 10, 1994.

Defense Science Board, *Report of the Defense Science Board Task Force on Readiness*, Washington, DC: Department of Defense, 94-S-2378, June 15, 1994.

Dertouzos, James N., *The Effects of Military Advertising: Evidence from the Advertising Mix Test*, Santa Monica, CA: RAND, N-2907-FMP, March 1989.

Dertouzos, James N., and Joseph E. Nation, *Manpower Structure and Policies in the United States and NATO Europe*, Santa Monica, CA: RAND, P-7608, January 1990.

Dertouzos, James N., J. M. Polich, A. Bamezai, and T. W. Chesnutt, *Recruiting Effects of Army Advertising*, Santa Monica, CA: RAND, R-3577-FMP, January 1989.

DeVany, Arthur S., Thomas R. Saving, and William F. Shughart, *Supply Rate and Equilibrium Inventory of Air Force Enlisted*

Personnel: A Simultaneous Model of the Accession and Retention Markets Incorporating Force Level Constraints, Brooks Air Force Base, TX: Air Force Human Resources Laboratory, AFHRL-TR-78-10, May 1978.

Dombyl, Karen N., *Unit Cohesion and Readiness: Implications for the Navy*, Alexandria, VA: Center for Naval Analyses, CRM 87-110, September 1987.

Fernandez, Richard L., and Jeffrey B. Garfinkle, *Setting Enlistment Standards and Matching Recruits to Jobs Using Job Performance Criteria*, Santa Monica, CA: RAND, R-3067-MIL, January 1985.

Fernandez, Richard L., Glenn A. Gotz, and Robert M. Bell, *The Dynamic Retention Model*, Santa Monica, CA: RAND, N-2141-MIL, April 1985.

Frankel, Oliver L., Robert A. Butler, and Margaret Carpenter-Huffman, *Army Manpower Cost System (AMCOS): Active Enlisted Force Prototype*, Arlington, VA: U.S. Army Research Institute for the Behavioral and Social Sciences, Technical Report 709, March 1986.

GRC International, Inc., *The Active Army Enlisted System Strength Management Decision Support System: Analyst's Training Course*, Manual, Vienna, VA, November 1, 1995.

Gabriel, Charles A., et al., *A Report On Military Capabilities and Readiness for United States Senator John S. McCain*, February 7, 1995.

Gorham, W., *Factors Affecting the Experience Composition of Airmen in USAF Job Categories: A Mathematical Approach*, Santa Monica, CA: RAND, RM-2144, January 30, 1958.

Gotz, Glenn A., and John J. McCall, *A Dynamic Retention Model for Air Force Officers: Theory and Estimates*, Santa Monica, CA: RAND, R-3028-AF, December 1984.

Gotz, Glenn A., and John J. McCall, *Estimating Military Personnel Retention Rates: Theory and Statistical Method*, Santa Monica, CA: RAND, R-2541-AF, June 1980.

Gotz, Glenn A., and Richard E. Stanton, *Modeling the Contribution of Maintenance Manpower to Readiness and Sustainability*, Santa Monica, CA: RAND, R-3200-FMP, January 1986.

Grissmer, David W., and Judith C. Fernandez, *Meeting Occupational and Total Manpower Requirements at Least Cost: A Nonlinear Programming Approach*, Santa Monica, CA: RAND, P-7123, July 1985.

Grissmer, David W., Sheila Nataraj Kirby, and Man-bing Sze, *Factors Affecting Reenlistment of Reservists: Spouse and Employer Attitudes and Perceived Unit Environment*, Santa Monica, CA: RAND, R-4011-RA, 1992.

Hall, Gaineford J., Jr., and S. Craig Moore, *Uncertainty in Personnel Force Modeling*, Santa Monica, CA: RAND, N-1842-AF, April 1982.

Halvorson, Colin O., "Readiness Baseline," briefing, Logistics Management Institute, McLean, VA, 1995.

Holz, Betty W., and Paul D. Phillips, *Improved Models to Measure Army Personnel Readiness*, McLean, VA: Research Analyses Corporation, Technical Paper RAC-TP-381, November 1969.

Horowitz, Stanley A., and Norma J. Hibbs, *Relating Resources to Readiness*, Alexandria, VA: Center for Naval Analyses, CNR 1, September 1979.

Hosek, James R., John Antel, and Christine E. Peterson, *Who Stays, Who Leaves? Attrition Among First-Term Enlistees*, Santa Monica, CA: RAND, N-2967-FMP, May 1989.

Hosek, James R., C. E. Peterson, J. VanWinkle, and H. Wong, *A Civilian Wage Index for Defense Manpower*, Santa Monica, CA: RAND, R-4190-FMP, 1992.

Hudson, Neff, "This One's For You: Perry's Package Would Put More Money In Your Pocket," *Air Force Times*, November 21, 1994, p. 14.

Hunt, Thomas R., *An Analysis of Proposed Changes to the U.S. Marine Corps Permanent Change of Station Policy: The Fiscal and Readiness Impacts*, Thesis, Naval Postgraduate School, Monterey, CA, March 1994.

James, Ulysses S., et al., *A Study of Systems Tools for Army Personnel Management*, Alexandria, VA: U.S. Army Research Institute for the Behavioral and Social Sciences, Research Note 83-48, December 1983.

Jaquette, David L., and Gary R. Nelson, *The Implications of Manpower Supply and Productivity for the Pay and Composition of the Military Force: An Optimization Model*, Santa Monica, CA: RAND, R-1451-ARPA, July 1974.

Jaquette, D. L., G. R. Nelson, and R. J. Smith, *An Analytic Review of Personnel Models in the Department of Defense*, Santa Monica, CA: RAND, R-1920-ARPA, September 1977.

Jones, G. T., *Army Turbulence and Strategic Readiness, 1992*, Carlisle Barracks, PA: U.S. Army War College, DTIC-AD-A264 234, April 15, 1993.

Kawata, Jennifer H., David W. Grissmer, and Richard Eisenman, *The Reserve Force Policy Screening Model (POSM): A User's Manual*, Santa Monica, CA: RAND, R-3701-JCS/RA/FMP, June 1989.

Kerce, Elyse W., *Quality of Life in the U.S. Marine Corps*, San Diego, CA: Navy Personnel Research and Development Center, NPRDC-TR-95-4, January 1995.

Kohler, Daniel F., *Using Survivor Functions to Estimate Occupation-Specific Bonus Effects*, Santa Monica, CA: RAND, March 1988.

Kralj, Mary M., Robert Sadacca, and Charlotte H. Campbell, *Definition and Measures of Individual and Unit Readiness and Family Phenomena Affecting It*, Alexandria, VA: U.S. Army Research Institute for the Behavioral and Social Sciences, ARI Research Note 91-32, February 1991.

Larson, Eric V., and Adele R. Palmer, *The Decisionmaking Context in the U.S. Department of the Navy: A Primer for Cost Analysts*, Santa Monica, CA: RAND, MR-255-PA&E, 1994.

Lockman, Robert F., *A Model for Predicting Recruit Losses*, Arlington, VA: Center for Naval Analyses, Professional Paper No. 163, 4 September 1976.

Lockman, Robert F., and Patrice L. Gordon, *A Revised Screen Model for Recruit Selection and Recruitment Planning*, Arlington, VA: Center for Naval Analyses, CRC 338, August 1977.

Marquis, M. Susan, and Sheila Nataraj Kirby, *Economic Factors in Reserve Attrition: Prior Service Individuals in the Army National Guard and Army Reserve*, Santa Monica, CA: RAND, R-3686-1-RA, March 1989.

Massey, H. G., *Introduction to the USAF Total Force Cost Model*, Santa Monica, CA: RAND, R-2098-AF, June 1977.

Matlick, Richard K., et al., *Cost and Training Effectiveness Analysis in the Army Life Cycle Systems Management Models*, Washington, DC: U.S. Army Research Institute for the Behavioral and Social Sciences, Technical Report 503, July 23, 1980.

Maxfield, Thomas R., *A Regression Model of the Effects of Personnel Characteristics on Aviation Readiness and Productivity*, Thesis, Naval Postgraduate School, Monterey, CA, December 1985.

Miller, Sidney H., Laura Critchlow Sammis, and Herbert J. Shukiar, *The Officer Force Progression Model: A Steady-State Mathematical Model of the U.S. Air Force Officer Structure*, Santa Monica, CA: RAND, R-1607-PR, November 1974.

Moore, S. Craig, J. A. Stockfisch, M. S. Goldberg, S. M. Holroyd, and G. G. Hildebrandt, *Measuring Military Readiness and Sustainability*, Santa Monica, CA: RAND, R-3842-DAG, 1991.

Mooz, W. E., and K. P. Heinze, *The Air Reserve Forces Study, Vol. X: Cost Analysis Methods and Procedures*, Santa Monica, CA: RAND, RM-5335-PR, October 1967.

Nakada, Michael K., *A Dynamic Model of Navy Enlisted Retention*, San Diego, CA: Navy Personnel Research and Development Center, NPRDC TR 84-20, February 1984.

National Defense Research Institute, *Assessing the Structure and Mix of Future Active and Reserve Forces: Final Report to the Secretary of Defense (Executive Summary)*, Santa Monica, CA: RAND, MR-140/2-OSD, 1993.

North, James H., et al., *Perspectives on Minority Officer Success Rates in the Marine Corps*, Alexandria, VA: Center for Naval Analyses, June 1994.

Orvis, Bruce R., H. J. Shukiar, Laurie McDonald, M. J. Mattock, M. R. Kilburn, and M. G. Shanley, *Ensuring Personnel Readiness in the Army Reserve Components*, Santa Monica, CA: RAND, MR-659-A, 1996.

Orvis, Bruce R., Michael T. Childress, and J. Michael Polich, *Effect of Personnel Quality on the Performance of Patriot Air Defense System Operators*, Santa Monica, CA: RAND, R-3901-A, 1992.

Orvis, Bruce R., Martin T. Gahart, and Alvin K. Ludwig, *Validity and Usefulness of Enlistment Intention Information*, Santa Monica, CA: RAND, R3775-FMP, 1992.

Palmer, Adele R., *Cost Factors in the Army: Vol. 1, The Decisionmaking Context*, Santa Monica, CA: RAND, R-4078/1-PA&E, 1992.

Palmer, Adele R., J. H. Bigelow, J. G. Bolten, D. Dizengoff, J. H. Kawata, H. G. Massey, R. L. Petruschell, and M. G. Shanley, *Assessing the Structure and Mix of Future Active and Reserve Forces: Cost Estimation Methodology*, Santa Monica, CA: RAND, MR-134-1-OSD, 1992.

Palmer, Adele R., and Eric V. Larson, *Cost Factors in the Army: Vol. 2, Factors, Methods, and Models*, Santa Monica, CA: RAND, R-4078/2-PA&E, 1992.

Palmer, Adele R., and C. Peter Rydell, *Developing Cost-Effectiveness Guidelines for Managing Personnel Resources in a Total Force Context: Executive Summary*, Santa Monica, CA: RAND, R-4005/2-FMP, 1991.

Palmer, Adele R., and C. Peter Rydell, *An Integrative Modeling Approach for Managing the Total Defense Labor Force*, Santa Monica, CA: RAND, R-3756-OSD/AF, December 1989.

Petruschell, Robert L., James H. Bigelow, and Joseph G. Bolten, *Overview of the Total Army Design and Cost System*, Santa Monica, CA: RAND, MR-195-A, 1993.

Polich, J. Michael, James N. Dertouzos, and S. James Press, *The Enlistment Bonus Experiment*, Santa Monica, CA: RAND, R-3353-FMP, April 1986.

Press, S. James, *Using the Pise Criterion to Measure the Effects of Imbalance in the Analysis of Covariance*, Santa Monica, CA: RAND, N-1890-MRAL, February 1983.

Quester, Alinc, et al., *National Manpower Inventory Final Report: Vols. I-III, Main Text, Technical Appendixes, Technical Documentation for Software for the Model*, Alexandria, VA: Center for Naval Analyses, CRC 533, September 1985.

Richards, Laurence D., Peter L. Eirich, and Murray A. Geisler, *A Concept for the Management of Readiness*, Washington, DC: Logistics Management Institute, January 1980.

Roane, Peter, Norma J. Hibbs, and Stanley A. Horowitz, *A Partial Review of the Literature Relating Resource Use to Readiness*, Arlington, VA: Center for Naval Analyses, (CNA)78-1128.10, August 15, 1978.

Roos, John G., "Redefining Readiness," *Armed Forces Journal International*, October 1994, pp. 33–42.

Rosenberg, Eric, "Grounding of Navy Jets Has Resulted in Worst Readiness Rating," *Defense Week*, December 5, 1994, p. 1.

Rosenberg, Eric, "Keeping Readiness High in the Navy Is a Concern," *Defense Week*, December 5, 1994, p. 7.

Rosenberg, Eric, "More Chinks in the Armor for Navy Aviation Readiness," *Defense Week*, December 12, 1994, p. 3.

Rosenberg, Eric, "Navy Has Plan to Predict Downturns in Readiness," *Defense Week*, December 12, 1994, p. 6.

Rostker, Bernard, *Air Reserve Personnel Study: Volume III, Total Force Planning, Personnel Costs, and the Supply of New Reservists*, Santa Monica, CA: RAND, R-1430-PR, October 1974.

Rydell, C. Peter, Adele R. Palmer, and David J. Osbaldeston, *Developing Cost-Effectiveness Guidelines for Managing Personnel*

Resources in a Total Force Context, Santa Monica, CA: RAND, R-4005/1-FMP, 1991.

Sadacca, Robert, Rodney A. McCloy, and Ani S. DiFazio, *The Impact of Army and Family Factors on Individual Readiness*, Alexandria, VA: U.S. Army Research Institute for the Behavioral and Social Sciences, Research Report 1643, August 1993.

Shishko, Robert, and Robert M. Paulson, *Relating Resources to the Readiness and Sustainability of Combined Arms Units*, Santa Monica, CA: RAND, R-2769-MRAL, December 1981.

Thompson, Theodore J., Iosif A. Krass, and Timothy T. Liang, *Quantifying the Impact of the Permanent Change of Station (PCS) Budget on Navy Enlisted Personnel Unit Readiness*, San Diego, CA: Navy Personnel Research and Development Center, TN-91-16, June 1991.

United States Department of Defense, Office of the Assistant Secretary of Defense, *Family Status and Initial Term of Service: Vol. I, Summary*, Washington, DC: December 1993.

United States Department of Defense, Office of the Assistant Secretary of Defense, *Family Status and Initial Term of Service: Vol. II, Trends and Indicators*, Washington, DC, December 1993.

United States Department of Defense, Office of the Assistant Secretary of Defense, *Family Status and Initial Term of Service: Vol. III, Field Study*, Washington, DC, December 1993.

United States Department of Defense, Office of the Assistant Secretary of Defense, *Family Status and Initial Term of Service: Vol. IV, Appendices*, Washington, DC, December 1993.

United States Department of Defense, Personnel Office of the Deputy Chief of Staff for Military Strength Analysis and Forecasting, *Information Briefing for Manpower and Personnel Executives*, Washington, DC, September 8, 1995.

United States General Accounting Office, *1995 Budget: Potential Reductions to the Operation and Maintenance Programs*, Washington, DC, GAO/NSIAD-94-246BR, September 1994.

United States General Accounting Office, *DOD Budget: Selected Categories of Planned Funding for Fiscal Years 1995–99*, Washington, DC, GAO/NSIAD-95-92, February 1995.

United States General Accounting Office, *DOD Force Mix Issues: Greater Reliance on Civilians in Support Roles Could Provide Significant Benefits*, Washington, DC, GAO/NSIAD-95-5, October 1994.

United States General Accounting Office, *Military Readiness, Mobilization Planning, and Civil Preparedness: Issues For Planning*, Washington, DC, PLRD-81-6, February 1981.

United States General Accounting Office, *Military Readiness: DOD Needs to Develop a More Comprehensive Measurement System*, Washington, DC, GAO/NSIAD-95-29, October 1994.

United States General Accounting Office, *Military Recruiting: More Innovative Approaches Needed*, Washington, DC, GAO/NSIAD-95-22, December 1994.

Van Nostrand, Sally J., et al., *Personnel Readiness Indicator Model (PRIM) Study*, Bethesda, MD: U.S. Army Concepts Analysis Agency, CAA-SR-84-5, September 1984.

Vernez, Georges, and Gail L. Zellman, *Families and Mission: A Review of the Effects of Family Factors on Army Attrition, Retention, and Readiness*, Santa Monica, CA: RAND, N-2624-A, August 1987.

Vicino, E. Byars, *Manpower and Training Research Information Systems (MATRIS): Summary Report*, San Diego, CA: Defense Technical Information Center, 1986.

Warner, John T., and Philip M. Lurie, *A Simulation of a New Model of Compensation and Retention*, Alexandria, VA: Center for Naval Analyses, (CNA) 79-1350, September 12, 1979.

Wild, William G., and Bruce R. Orvis, *Design of Field-Based Crosstraining Programs and Implications for Readiness*, Santa Monica, CA: RAND, R-4242-A, 1993.

Williams, Robert H., "Industry Leader Sounds Preparedness Warning," *National Defense*, December 1994, p. 18.